The Incarnation from White Glacier Mountain

(The Biography of Gangkar Rinpoche)

By Minyag Gonpo

Translated by S. Brinson Aldridge

ISBN 978-0-7414-4585-8

Published by:

INFIN∞ITY
PUBLISHING.COM

1094 New DeHaven Street, Suite 100
West Conshohocken, PA 19428-2713
Info@buybooksontheweb.com
www.buybooksontheweb.com
Toll-free (877) BUY BOOK
Local Phone (610) 941-9999
Fax (610) 941-9959

Printed in the United States of America

Published December 2013

Table of Contents

List of Illustrations

All photos by Brinson Aldridge except as noted

Translator's Preface

This book is the story of Gangkar Rinpoche, a remarkable Buddhist teacher from the part of the eastern Tibetan plateau called Kham-Minyak. The Minyak Tibetan group which gives this region of Kham its name has had a significant role in the history of Kham and Amdo, the area to the north. Gangkar Rinpoche was responsible, during the 1930s and 1940s, for the revival of centers of learning in Minyak famous throughout Kham and Amdo. He is also renowned as a Minyak native for tirelessly teaching and spreading knowledge of Tibetan culture. His students would come to Minyak from all over Tibet and China, and would be influential in introducing Tibetan Buddhism to the West. His legacy continues today in China in the teaching of Tibetan culture in universities, printing and translation of rare Tibetan books and art, and research collaboration with Tibetologists worldwide.

The "White Lotus of Confidence," the second part of the title of the "Biography of the White Galcier Mountain Incarnation" and another way of referring to the biography, is a recent publication. It is not long by some standards, but is the first account of any length of the man known as the Gangkar incarnation. Although it is a hagiography, the biography of a saint, it does not follow the format of many more traditional "life-stories" (rnam thar). The reasons for this approach are explained by the author.

For those who may have traveled on the Tibetan plateau in the last 20-30 years and have observed the economic, social and environmental changes in the Eastern (Kham) and Northeastern Tibetan regions (Amdo), he or she will know it is easy to find biographies of Tibetan Buddhist teachers among the many publications available in marketplace stalls and bookstores selling classic Tibetan texts alongside modern novels, short stories and textbooks. This translation

iii

of a modern Tibetan book with a new approach to the spiritual biography genre makes another example of contemporary Tibetan writing available to readers in the West.

Bo Gangkar is the Minyak name given to the 17th highest peak in the world, located at the southern end of the Great Snow Mountains (Da Xue Shan) in southwest China. Bo ('Bo) means "mountain" in Minyak language and the Tibetan word Gangkar (gangs-dkar) means "white glacier." From the Tibetan word Gangkar we get the Chinese name Gonga Shan (mountain). The story of Gangkar Rinpoche cannot be separated from that of the Buo-pa or Minyak people who live near the mountain, the Kham-Minyak region in which he was born and raised. In this part of Kham monasteries belonging to all the major Tibetan Buddhist traditions could be found.

I am a student of Buddhist teachers in the Nyingma-Kagyu lineages of Tibetan Buddhism, the same lineages in which Gangkar Rinpoche received his training and ones I share with the author of this biography, Minyak Gonpo. For many years I have been traveling on pilgrimage to sacred Buddhist sites in Asia. I do this for inspiration and to deepen the connection with the practice lineages of my Buddhist teachers. Encouraged by my Tibetan teachers to travel to China, I have collected pilgrim guide books written in Tibetan. My interests in meditation and visiting caves, mountain retreats, and temples where Buddhist masters have practiced in the past has been inspired by reading these Tibetan guidebook descriptions of the benefits in meditation practice from visiting sacred sites. Important places in Buddhist pilgrimage are associated with hills or mountains much of the time so usually the goal of my travels has been clusters of sacred mountains, starting with those regarded as most sacred in both the Chinese and Tibetan traditions. The biography of Gangkar Rinpoche has helped me value the recent history of areas visited on pilgrimage in Kham.

On one visit to Kham in 1999 I was invited to look at the books in a private library near Dege. While browsing books over a week, I found my first references to Minyak, a most excellent place it was written for study and meditation, particularly near the mountain, Gangkar. When I was traveling out of Kham and stopped by the giant stupa at a major crossroads at Xinduqiao on the road to Kangding, I saw the word Minyak written on the sign marking the name of the stupa. I met several monks who told me they were from monasteries in Minyak located out in the valleys to the south. I was determined to learn more about Minyak and to travel there. An article in a Tibetan magazine by Minyak Gonpo increased my interest even more. My enthusiasm spurred me to translate the article about Minyak for friends (included in the appendices).

On my next visit to China, I was fortunate to meet Gonpo. I soon began to read his new book about his teacher, Gangkar Rinpoche. I was able to return to Beijing in 2001 and have a series of meetings with Gonpo to discuss my reading of his Gangkar Rinpoche biography. Gonpo's explanations, anecdotes, and patience with my many questions made the context for names of people, places, and events mentioned in the book possible. Sustaining my work on a draft of the biography in English was the occasional break during my stay in Beijing to seek out sacred caves and temples in the city limits or hills to the West. These breaks complemented the inspiration I found in reading the pilgrimage guide to places in Minyak included in the biography of Gangkar Rinpoche. I learned even more about Minyak when I discussed visits to Minyak made in the 40's with two elderly monks now living on the island of Putuo Shan, sacred to Kwanyin (Avalokitesvara), located off the China coast near Shanghai. It was at Putuo Shan that plans to go to Minyag came into focus.

A word about the spelling of Tibetan names: names of people and places that are widely used in the press and books about Tibet are presented in transliterated form, following the pronunciation of the name. Examples are Karmapa, Gangkar, and Minyak. For all other names, the original Tibetan spelling in Wylie transcription is used for the sake of historical accuracy, except for Chinese names written in Tibetan which have been converted to *pinyin* spelling. Transcribed Tibetan names are displayed with the first pronounced syllable capitalized. For example "lama" is spelled bla-ma in Tibetan, so with the first letter pronounced it would be transcribed as bLa-ma. Some Tibetan words can be be transferred directly with no changed such as the name Lhasa. In the conversion to *pinyin*, more people will recognize the capital of Sichuan, Chengdu, in its *pinyin* form rather than Khrin-tu in Tibetan transcription. There are a few Chinese names spelled out in Tibetan rather than Chinese *pinyin* in cases where those helping me with the conversion from Tibetan spelling were not sure of the *pinyin* spelling. The original text has the spelling of names and places in other languages, all in Tibetan letters. I recognize that having different spelling conventions in the translation is a challenge, and I ask for the reader's indulgence in how I chose to respond to the variety of spelling forms in the original Tibetan text. I have tried to keep with standard Wylie transcription as the default.

Since the original book in Tibetan was written for a small audience of Kagyu disciples of Gangkar Rinpoche, students of Kham and Minyak history, three sections have been added as appendices, one providing more background on Minyak and Tibetan Buddhist sects in Kham, intended for the non-specialist; the second a translation of Minyak Gonpo's article on Minyag, a major inspiration for this project; and the third notes on a visit to Minyak in 2003 which will be of interest to those taking the route to Gangkar monastery via the Yulungxi valley. For those who are familiar with traditional Tibetan Buddhist biographies, the appendices can be read later. Others reading about Kham or a spiritual biography of a Tibetan Buddhist teacher for the first time may wish to start with the appendices. Books on Tibetan history by Richardson, Snellgrove, Stein, Kapstein and others are also highly recommended (see suggested reading) for those wishing to deepen their understanding of background events mentioned in the biography.

For those who read Tibetan and obtain a copy of the Gangkar biography in Tibetan, I have included the page numbers of the original text in brackets. Another use of brackets is for the addition of wording in English that is not automatically assumed to be present in the Tibetan, but allows for a better rendering of the meaning in English.

I also have included the Tibetan for philosophical terms or yogic processes. In the translation itself, I have retained the original chapter headings in bold type.

The pilgrimage guide by Gangkar Rinpoche has been presented in a bi-lingual format, Tibetan on the left page with English on the right facing page. My journey to Minyak in 2003 (described in the appendices) only scratched the surface. As is often the case when exploring glaciated, high-altitude terrain, many of the trails to places described in the guide were washed out when I

was there and time did not allow for extended detours to visit the sites. I would like to revisit the area and hope that others can further document the current state of many of the places mentioned in the guide, some of which I was able to view only with the aid of binoculars from higher altitude.

As Gonpo has said, he hopes that the Gangkar biography will be corrected where errors exist and be a foundation for compiling a more complete biography of Gangkar Rinpoche. I hope this translation may serve as one resource for this task.

I am inspired by the stories of Gangkar Rinpoche's selfless dedication to helping others through teaching. His legacy is clearly visible in the devotion and commitment of his students to restoring the monasteries in Minyak and continuing with research in Tibetan studies. Minyak is one of the most beautiful parts of Kham. If reading this book moves others to travel to Minyak and visit temples, monasteries and other sacred sites there, then the benefit in increasing knowledge about the good people of Minyak and the legacy of Gangkar Rinpoche might compensate for shortcomings in a Buddhist layman's attempts at scholarship.

Acknowledgments

This translation would not have been possible without the kindness and support of Gonpo. Gonpo opened his home to me and made time to answer many questions about people and places mentioned in the biography. We first began our regular meetings at his home in Beijing several times a week in late 2001. The warmth, generosity and patience of Gonpo, the kindness of his wife, Chodron, and assistance of his children will never be forgotten. I was constantly amazed by Gonpo's energy, his ability to speed-walk across the street, and committments to regular meetings at the Minorties National Library, long after his official retirement. He was relaxed and tireless in his work with teachers at the monasteries in Minyak. In 2003 my wife and I traveled there with Gonpo, Chodron, and one of his daughters, Sonam Dolma. Gonpo took us to Gangkar Rinpoche's birthplace, to the temple where Rinpoche's relics are enshrined, and arranged for our journey by horseback to Gangkar monastery.

My deep gratitude goes to my good friend, Zhang Ji Chuan, Tibetan scholar and linguist, who introduced me to Gonpo, for his energetic support for this project.

Many other people in China and Minyak have contributed indirectly to the translation project, mKhan-po mDo-sngags bsTan-pa'i Nyi-ma of Khams-gsum grags monastery, the monks who led our party on horse over the passes to Gang-dkar Monastery from the mother monastery of Khams-gsum grags, and members of Gonpo's family who welcomed us into their homes in Minyak.

Thanks also go to Kham Aid Foundation, with projects to preserve murals at monasteries throughout Kham and recently-discovered ancient murals found in Minyak homes, for their support of this translation project.

Thanks to my good friends Rick Geggie for sharing the struggle of writing while working on his book, and retreats in high-altitude environments in the White Mountains of California; Beimin Ni for support on work with pilgrimage; Professor Michael Saso, for his insight and deep knowledge into the cultures of minority peoples in Kham; and Scott Hajicek-Dobberstein for editing and translation.

It has not been easy to work full-time as a network engineer and find the blocks of time to work on the translation and background materials for this book. I take full responsibility for all errors and omissions. The views in the appendices, except for the translation of the Minyak history article, are my own. This project has taken six years, including two pilgrimages to Kham and study in Beijing. None of it would have been possible if not for the support and patience of my family and my partner, So San.

New Year's Day, Year of the Earth Mouse, 2008
Oakland, California

The Incarnation From White Glacier Mountain

('Bo Gangs dkar sprul-sku'i rnam-thar dad-pa'i pad-dkar bzhugs)

(The White Lotus of Confidence,
the Spiritual Biography of Gangkar Rinpoche)

By

Minyak Gonpo

Translated from the Tibetan
S.Brinson Aldridge

Table of Contents and page number (indicated by number enclosed in brackets in translation) in original Tibetan text

[1] **Praises**

Na mo guru dharma siddha ye!

I take refuge in the reality of all awakened ones of the three
   times, my master, pure and great, rDo-rje 'chang,
   precious root teacher.

I follow you in all times and circumstances.

Although resting in tranquility, he does not dwell on the edge
   of that tranquility.
Although living in cyclic existence, he is free of the pollution
   in such life.
Precious Buddhist teachings, the proper explanation
   reflecting the intentions of the Victorious One, fall as
   a rain of maxims.
With the brilliance of the lord who brings light, his form
   emerged from the water treasure of two limitless
   accumulations;
The hosts of stars that emerged pretending to the greatness of
   this temple,
Have rested peacefully, unchanged, for some time.

The elephant of the realm dwells in the middle of the heart
   and given courage to speak through the glory in
   spiritual teachings.
Like a lion amid a herd of complaining cattle

[2] Evil views that reside in the heart are cast out completely
    down to one's very bones.
With the words of Buddha and most excellent sons of the
    Victorious One,
All the aphorisms, properly commented upon, are held as
    nourishment deep in my heart.
With advice on all experiences that one can have,
Sensitive to thoughts in the minds of all sentient beings
With a mother's kindness,
You, a lion among men of the Minyak region,
All-knowing teacher, I regard as the best of them all.
On the petals of a pure white lotus of confidence,
The pollen tears', like strings of pearls,
Small drops fall to a spot at the base.
In the shade of the ten petals, they quickly vanish.
This unending spiritual biography: who can recount it all?
A few scattered memories…
I offer a brief record.

It is difficult to list the names of my root teacher here. Gangs-dkar rDo-rje 'chang Ka-rma bShad-sgrub Chos-kyi Seng-ge's heart-mind[1] dissolved into the "vast expanse of meaningfulness" (chos dbyings) on the 28th day of 12th month in the Fire-Monkey year of the 16th cycle (Jan 28, 1957). It appears that over forty years have passed since then.

In 1957 I became a teacher at the Southwest Nationalities University, on the 5th day of 3rd month in the Western calendar (March 5). Alas! Into the deep waters of the heart, suddenly a rain of stones falls. As if stirred up from the depths, each wave joining, contending with the next, this stick[2] that stirs up the depths of the mind, is it made of metal or stone? When I heard the bad news that my kind teacher had passed into *nirvana* (shi-ba) the grief I felt then is, even now, a clear image in my heart. By that the connection between student and teacher is clearly shown. But at the time I did not dare to speak of the circumstances of my teacher's passing or to write a spiritual biography. [4] I had no choice but to not show my feelings, as if there were no bad conditions or anything besides a peaceful, happy, pleasant time in this world.

Even so, I had studied with him uninterruptedly for 28 years. From all of his students he ranked me as the best. When requesting vows of a layman, I was given the name Ka-rma Chos-grub Seng-ge, a large part of his own name. When I (first) would go to his small dormitory, I used a broken pot on the stove most of the time, and lacked decent clothing or bedding. I was constantly asking about the meaning of the texts. He always offered me butter, cheese and the like and provided me with monk's garments. During periods of practice he would compliment me many times, calling me "Sha-ri-bu, the most excellent of the wise." He gave me practice texts and loaned me the best books that belonged to his own teacher. Many times he even gave me the clothing worn by his teacher. My teacher had a loving kindness greater than that of my own parents. Now it came to a time when I would never again see him, gone as he had to the vast expanse of peace.

For many months the tears did not dry on my face. There seemed no way of clearing up my gloomy spirits. Until now, in dreams I see the pleasant face of my teacher and listen to him, dreaming of him hundreds, thousands of times. When I have dreams like this, following each dream, the smiling face of my teacher appears clearly in my mind for many days. The sound of his melodious speech is vividly present. But since these are mistaken appearances where is the ultimately real? [5]

"The student without a teacher,
A child without parents,
Three little boats without a lead:
Where do you go, not knowing, driven by karma?"

Recently, a most excellent person who was not only highly disciplined but an expert, the late sKyid-gling mChog-sprul,[3] asked me many times, and wrote in a letter sent with a gift, "write a book, a spiritual biography of our teacher." Even many "dharma brothers" scattered around the world have asked me repeatedly to do this. But I have no desire to just imitate others so carry on with my own work; it is difficult to meet the expectations of all who have encouraged me in this effort.

Generally speaking, the word rnam-thar means envisioning the structure (rnam) of a composition and being able to put in print the seed of or to set out on the path of liberation (thar). But for one like me who has all sorts of fetters, embodied in the swamp of cyclic existence, dull-minded, how can one say that I will achieve a goal such as this?[4]

However, I have looked through nearly a thousand spiritual biographies of all sorts, large and small, of the pundits of

India, great adepts (*siddhas*), translators and scholars of Tibet, teachers who were both creative and accomplished holy persons. In the spiritual biographies of persons from a thousand years ago mention is made of when a person was born and died and how many years he (or she) lived; scholars make different claims. Not only is it said that master Nagajuna lived for 500 years, but [6] there are other issues which one can question [such as those] shown in the different years that have been recorded for the dates of the birth and death of one high lama of Tibet, Gongs-pa rab-gsal, and for the translator Rin-chen bzang-po.

Still, there is a pattern of there being a period of time [from the death before] one or more students write the spiritual biography of a teacher. First, I read many books, the sayings of the Victorious One,[5] hidden treasure texts of well-known revealers of such books, and the collected works of the great adepts of China and Tibet. While (reading) I would find words that "my lama has a title such as this or one aspect of him is like this" stating "my lama is a victorious, perfected awakened one (Buddha)" or "he was a holy person supported by tradition" or "there was a prophecy by such and such discoverer of texts or great adept." Or he had achieved awakening after innumerable eons and the [book has been] written because he had developed the most excellent pure and total mind and had made salutations and worship to Buddhas and *bodhisattvas*. For a long time [stories were] were written like this to amaze people. Along these lines the writers declare, for sure, that the subject is the emanation of some awakened being of India, a *bodhisattva*, one of the 80 *siddhas*, six jewels,[6] or two excellence ones.[7] In addition a link with the sacred is made by stating that there is a connection because [the teacher] is the incarnation or rebirth of one of the five founders of the Sakyapa in Tibet; of one of the three, Marpa, Milarepa, or Gampopa; the teacher Padmasambhava or Longchen Rabjampa, or one of the well-known realized masters. Those with sharp horns of sectarian bias [7] hide behind a vast expanse of obfuscation. If individual philosophies and instructions are discussed, the view, contemplation and application of [the lama's] philosophical system are said to be deeper and higher than any other. And even if the view of some philosophical system is directly in tune with Sakyamuni, it is stated that this was not clearly explained by the six gems, or the two excellent ones and every Tibetan teacher before did not understand it. But now the explanation is based on a realized understanding. If one looks at what is said, these are like praises for the teacher. As to the real meaning, taking "my teacher" out of the words, praise is revealed as just a disservice to what is real.

Still, in some spiritual biographies and books, strings of words express qualities through fine embellishment, using poetry, with expressions such as "like a garland, pleasing, emanating light". These poetic expressions are sweet to the ear; some have made it into dictionaries compiled in the analysis of how words are used. If one considers the inner meaning of what is said, sometimes it is a thorn of sectarianism that comes out right away or sometimes the solitary, but loud, voice of one pretending to be learned. Because there is no sticking to the facts, when trying to decide if something is true or not, much of the time one is just left with not being certain of much of anything.

Especially the ones who, thinking only of the benefits of their own school of thought, tell a story of how, with head bowed, they gave up life before some butcher, a captain of evil troops coming through from another country, hands red with the blood of tens of thousands of Tibetans, create a great hill of praise for themselves: all are like wolves in sheep's' clothing.[8] [8] Those who, for the sake of their own group, make disputes and conflict without regard for life are like a thorn in the heart, regard enemies with a deep anger like something caught in one's eye, acting with no dignity. If one reads some of these [books], such as at the beginning of gYung ston rdo-rje dpal's auto-biography, the biography by the student uses forceful language and dismisses the teacher as mostly a charlatan. On the other hand, in their own spiritual biographies, having abandoned exaggeration and disparagement, they write little. Where do they take responsibility in what they say?

If spiritual biographies of some great scholars and translators of the past are read by spiritual practitioners, though it is possible that these works are merely the praises of shopkeepers and ordinary people, practitioners will feel a bit ashamed that someone was compelled to write them. For example, in the story of Bari Lotsawa it is said that "he offered half an ounce of gold as an initiation price to the teacher rDo-rje gdan-pa, and offered the three: fees, drink, and cloth.[9] The teacher said that those gifts were not enough. When he offered an additional half-ounce of gold and six more fees, drink, and cloth, the teacher was happy and gave the complete instruction."

In a biography of Atisa one reads: "Once the 'Great Lord' was staying at Sol-nag thang-bo- che. There were about 1000 monks for Khu-ston and not more than 300 masters and servants for Atisa. Requests and needs were few for Atisa. Since nothing unusual was happening, right away Atisa said with disgust: "Khu-ston is like a universal emperor. I am an ordinary person. Khu-ston is like the 33 sensuous enjoyments.[10] [9] I am a hungry ghost." During the evening, after consultation with Brom-ston, Atisa ran away to Nye-thang." And in an old Sa-skya-pa text it says: "Sa-chen Kun-dga' snying-po went to the translator Mar to request teachings. In order to choose those who were ready to receive teachings, translator Mar did not given him any instruction except for a little from the "Discourses" (Tshogs bshad). Because he saw many poor people and seekers of spiritual instruction on the road as he was returning, Sa-chen then offered 80 ounces of gold as an initiatory offering at the feet of Mar Lotsawa. Mar was delighted and gave him the complete instruction."

9

In some texts that discuss the cycle of 'Jigs-byed it is said that: "Rva Lotsawa wanted a full ounce of gold for each 'Jigs-byed empowerment. The translator sMon-lam grags offered only one ounce of gold, so Rva-lo did not include the empowerment of the six lineages (gdong drug). Therefore [the full] 'Jigs-byed empowerment was not given."

In a spiritual biography of Rva-lo it says that when he went to Lho-brag to teach at the request of a benefactor, Marpa's son, Dar-ma mdo-sde, came there. People paid more respect to Dar-ma mdo-sde than to Rva-lo. Rva-lo became angry and said: "I am the translator who went south to Nepal. Since you are here merely to teach Tibetans, there is no purpose in just standing around like this. Let us two debate the teachings." Dar-ma mdo-sde said: "I am a practitioner of the Father-Son Buddha teaching lineage. I am not like you who trusts in just evil spells and dark deeds." Rva-lo became very angry at this and uttered a black magic spell: "Kill Da-rma mdo-sde." Rva-lo's words became famous in a song: "He killed thirteen heroes who had reached the spiritual level, led by one son, Da-rma mdo-sde; [10] although he went to hell when he died, he had no regret."

If one reads what has been written, these scholars and translators (seem to) have jealous and angry minds. They are sellers of the *vajrayana* teachings. A businessman is an ordinary person, only more interested in money (than others). Why should we not question what others write, for the sake of status and their reputations, about throwing blood on a Buddha-image, or about brave individuals who have reached some spiritual level? These holy people can't be like that; everyone clearly understands this. But sacred teachings and images are up for sale these days and support those merchants looking for a profit.

Among the spiritual biographies by disciples, those that have an elegant style like the biography of Milarepa are very rare. In that biography a young lad is weak, abandoned as a child.

All the series of events that he went through to become a great *siddha* known throughout the world have been written down. In those stages the deep love and connection between mother and son, brother and sister is clearly described. Also, wild actions made in anger, at the spur of the moment, and those bad changes in his life brought on by enemies are described. In the end, because of fierce determination, how these enemies were overcome is detailed. Intensely ashamed of all [the wrong] he had done to improve his circumstances when his life was at a low point, he served a qualified teacher. Though rebuked and sent away by his teacher he saw his teacher as, in reality, an awakened being, so he bore hardship with courage. He obtained the complete instructions and in the end reached the ultimate goal.

[11] Here, if one perseveres despite difficulties, not only can we say that it is true that all action produces a result, but also that spiritual teachings (*dharma*) and the world are in contradiction, like fire and water. It is said that if one is to become successful in a worldly sense, a spiritually meaningful life will not result. If one is to be devoted to *dharma* then it is necessary to give up the world. One might say there is no contradiction between the world and spiritual values, but relying on what is spiritual (chos) is completely different from the concerns of those who seek a worldly life. Still, out of all the many autobiographies (rang rnam) of kLong-chen Rab-'byams, Jonang Taranatha, Panchen bLo-bzang Chos-rgyan, Situ Chos-kyi Byung-gnas, Zhu-chen Tshul-khrums Rin-chen and so forth, each writes in a uncomplicated way with few superfluous words. There is little talk of seeing gods or ghosts; there are specific spiritual teachings, no make believe. When I look at the autobiography of 'Brug-pa Kun-legs, this is an extraordinary autobiography.[11] Topics covered there clearly reveal, in all their transparency, the basic shortcomings of false practitioners. He could criticize them since his conduct, good or bad, was transparent (naked), not hidden or secret. If practice of *dharma* is to be completely pure, what one must do to be in accord with this is to be very clear in the discussion of spiritual practice. This is as rare as [seeing] a star during the daytime. Suppose the holy scholar rDzogs-chen dPal-sprul had written his autobiography. Although it is certain it would have been written elegantly, it seems there was no time for him to do so. None has been found up to now.

[12] Nowadays our new generation of scholars is developing. They live loyal to the people, free of the traps and limitations of philosophical positions in spiritual traditions. They know the written languages of many peoples and countries, are free of narrow mindedness or attachment to what is old, with a wider outlook. In support, ultimately, of the thoughts and hopes of each of them, this is my effort, with no thought beyond just that. Nowadays (scholars) write many journals and other works. The essays stick to the facts, are easy to understand, with clear wording, bearing the special characteristics of this time, a strong connection with real life. One could say that for us Tibetans a new tradition of writing has opened up. But, drawing on the good parts of our elders mentioned above and writers both inside and outside our country, it is important to expand on a tradition of writing that reflects the special characteristics of our people. Although we are free of one set of fetters, we might find ourselves with another. It is very important that this not happen, that, as is said, "The lamb escaped the fox but met the tiger."

It is not difficult to write a general rough outline of Gangkar Rinpoche's life with prayers of the lineage and teachings of previous root teachers, an abbreviated "seed" spiritual biography, or comprehensive calendar based on a diary of the times before he died. Because of the way things have degenerated these days, source documents, even down to a single letter, have been destroyed and not even thought about. Having abandoned the make believe by relying on my root teacher for 28 years, I have pretended to write a little, using a style of brief remembrances (rjes dran).

[13] I am weakened by the burden of my many years. The strength in my five senses has run down and my memory is faulty. It is difficult to fulfill expectations of those who have encouraged me. Having written these sections of a general biography of my teacher, may readers not find too many faults with the writing!

Not having been separated from the limits of what I know through study,
And not having tamed the wild yak of my mind through thinking,
Brother of the parrot chattering in the forest of subtle points in traditional learning,
I have said too much.

[14] The previous lineages and the origin of the title of Gangs-dkar bla-ma (White Glacier Teacher)

Among four great glaciated mountains, well-known throughout Tibet, is a hidden region in the east: Gangs-dkar. It is between the Nyag-chu (Yalong) and the rGyal-mo dngul-chu[12] (Tadu) Rivers, near Dar-rtse-mdo and the center of Minyak ring-mo. Dar-rtse (or rtsi)-mdo is a Minyak word. *Dar* is silk and *rtsi* a word for medicine. Dartsendo (Dar-rtse-mdo) gets its name because it was a juncture (mdo) where the trade in medicine and silk took place between Tibet and China. Gangs-dkar peak is 7800[13] meters above sea level. To the scientists of more than ten countries and mountaineers who have climbed it, it is one of the great peaks in the world and its fame is emphasized again and again in the traditions starting from the teacher Padmasambhava, the *dakini* Yeshe Tsogyal and so on. There are many meditation caves, special, sacred sites. Surrounding (nye-skor) the venerable Tara's site are images of 21 Taras that have appeared by themselves out of solid rock. At the rDo-rje phag-mo (Vajravarahi) site a thousand Buddha images have appeared by themselves on a rock face with colorful illumination. The images, mantra, praises of the qualities of rDo-rje phag-mo are sculpted in relief.

[15] The area is filled with signs of spiritual achievement, the hand and foot prints of 80 Indian siddhas, Guru Rinpoche and his 25 disciples, Lha-lung dpal-rdor and many Karmapas. The major sites are imbued with the sustaining power from many magical manifestations that appeared when local (malignant) spirits were crushed under the feet of great *siddhas* such as the master among yogis, gNyis-med rDo-rje, master of accomplishment, Kun-dga' rGyal-mtshan, and the adept, Thang-stong rGyal-po.

Thang-stong rGyal-po

In the middle of the 13th century, at the end of the 4th Tibetan calendrical cycle, dPal Ara Chos-rje rGyal-mtshan, one of three adepts, built a small retreat house at Minyak rab-sgang, past the last of Srong-btsan sGam-po's series of temples.[14] Later a nephew of Ara Chos-rje, bLa-ma Grags-pa'i dPal, added on to the meditation house of his teacher and established a kind of mountain retreat (ri-khrod). As the number of those doing retreats and pilgrims increased, the mountain retreat was called White Glacier Monastery. bLa-ma Grags-pa'i dpal got the name Gangkar Lama (White

Glacier Teacher). With that, the lineage of the Gangkar teachers started.

Gangkar Lama Grags-pa'i dPal was born in the Iron-Monkey year of the 4 cycle (1260). By 1285, in the 5th cycle, during the Wood–Bird year, when he was 26, he had established the Gangkar practice place. He was able to significantly expand the tradition of (meditation) practice when the adept Karma Paksi traveled throughout Kham and 'Jang (Yunnan). He brought together 500 sharp-witted monks who became most excellent students and were able to understand and apply the doctrines they were studying.

[16] Second in the succession, rMa-se sTon-pa Rin-chen bzang-po was born in the Fire-Snake year (1317) of the 5th calendrical cycle into the rMa-se tribe at eastern Minyak ring-mo. He took vows with the bLa-ma bSod-nams rGyal-mtshan. He sought many empowerments and instructions and studied deep spiritual teachings with Minyak sages such as bLa-ma sNying-po rGyal-mtshan and 'Jam-dbyangs Ye-shes rDo-rje. When he was 18, in the Wood-Dog year of the 6th calendrical cycle (1334), he was made an assistant to bLa-ma 'Jam-dbyangs Ye-shes rDo-rje. Later they went on pilgrimage (grva skor) to dBu-tsang. On the way they met Master Rang-byung rDo-rje as he was coming down from his upper palace. They followed him to dBus lha-ldan (Lhasa) and studied many deep teachings of the oral transmission with the master himself, such as the root text and commentary to the Profound Inner Meaning. Then they toured the sacred places of dBu-tsang: secret caves, sNye-thang, ancient sites at Zhva-lu, sNar-thang, Jo-nang, 'Bri-gung and those of the 'Brug-pa (Kagyu) and Sa-skya-pa lineages. He requested non-sectarian teachings from Lord Bu-ston Rinpoche, the Jo-nang Kun-mkhyen, and the Sa-skya-pa scholar dBang-phyug dPal. He stayed in dBu-tsang for more than 15 years, staying mainly with the Jo-nang kun-mkhyen bla-ma, spending 12 years in a Kalacakra retreat gaining experience with the six applications.[15] Among those known as the Jo-nang-pa four "great sons" (bu-chen), rMa-se sTon-pa was the leading "great son." When he was close to

returning, he requested the complete teachings and all spiritual practices for Vajrayogini from Trepopa, who had a realized understanding. He had a very good connection with this teacher who gave him a very nice image of Maitreya made from red copper.

[17] In his 36th year, in the Water-Dragon year of the 6th calendrical cycle (1352), he returned to Rab sgang and stayed at bSam-'grub Rin-chen gLing. He lived on gifts of money and food. Though he kept his ritual observances to a single residence, he took care of students who studied with him. Through specific and detailed explanation on the teaching of action and its result, people everywhere were able to open their eyes to what to accept or reject. He was able to mediate any disturbances that arose. He built a new temple, Ra-ti Dar-rgyas. He turned over the responsibility of the monastery (gdan sa) to the Professor Shakya dPal. When he reached his 60th year, in the Water-Mouse Year of the 6th calendrical cycle (1372), in dreams he saw that he had all sorts of good connections with a place in Eastern Minyak ring-mo, a single day's journey by horse from 'Bo Gangs-dkar. At the convergence of the rMu-rgyu and 'Khro-'dzi valleys, from where the ancestors of Tibetan tribes[16] branched-out, behind the mountain at Gar-mi-sked-pa, at Cakrasamvara's place, he established a monastery. This also bore the name of the first monastery there called rMa-se dgon Khams-gsum-rags bde-chen gling. Its fame spread like the wind.[17] Later, he stayed on at this monastery and built a college and practice facilities. Teaching expanded greatly. Besides those already there [the number of] students increased to about 600. He was made the master of rMa-se monastery and the old Gangkar monastery, continuing to live a life of contemplation.

[18] After the establishment of the monastery, four years later in the Wood-Rabbit Year (1374), the Lord Karmapa Rol-pa'i rdo-rje came there from his upper palace. He came to pay homage to Minyak rab-sgang.[18] He mediated many disputes at Rab-sgang and gave spiritual teachings to the Minyak

(people) with rMa-se sTon-pa serving as his translator. The master Karmapa stayed for more than two months and completed all that was requested of him. When it came time for the Karmapa to leave, he gave him (rMa-se) a fine image that he had brought with him from his upper residence. He was advised: "May you return soon to the monastery (rMa-se). May your practice be most excellent!" Whenever the Karmapa returned, he made his retreats only at rMa-se monastery. rMa-se ston-pa died on the morning of the 20th day of 11 month, in the Water-Pig year of the 6th cycle, having reached 67 years old (1383).

Rma-se rTogs-ldan bLo-gros Rin-chen was born in the Fire-Tiger year of the 6th calendrical cycle (1386) in the region of Minyak Gha. (Nowadays this is associated with people of sKye-rgu-mdo, mTsho-sngon (Qinghai). sKye-rgu-mdo is a Minyak term for a place where rivers converge. The original Minyak term is Cu-sngon-'dus). He was a "heart-son" to Master Karmapa De-bzhin-gsheg-pa. He increased the teaching of the practice lineage and later became quite famous. He was born four years after the passing of rMa-se ston-pa, but don't confuse (his life story) because of some similarities in the lineage.

The 3rd in succession was Ka-rma Chos-kyi 'Od-zer. During his reign and during that of the 4th in the lineage, Ka-rma kun-dga' dpal, the teachings spread widely. Yet the evil armies of the Sog, O, Rod, and Tsho came into mTsho-sngon (Qinghai) and parts of Kham. By the time they came to 'Jang, they had been to eastern Minyak ring-mo many times. They burned, killed, plundered many villages, destroying everything.

[19] All the original teachings of Minyak were destroyed when the printing house at rMa-se monastery was wrecked. The community was diminished following the destruction of the monastery. The Buddhist teachings in Minyak were damaged, the (opportunity) to listen to the stories about the culture lost. A dark time came lasting about 300 years. The succession in this time was broken. We can reckon that the 5th in the succession, Karma bDe-gshegs was born at rGyal-mo Tsha-ba-rong in the 17th century, at the beginning of the 11th calendrical cycle. The 6th in the succession was Ka-rma Byang-chub bsTan-'dzin, born at dGu-rong dzong shar-kha-rong. The 7th in the line, Ka-rma 'Jigs-med was born in the region called 'Bo-log, nowadays Shis-khrung khongs[19] (prefecture). The 8th, Karma Tshe-ring dBang-po was born near the monastery at rMu-rgyu zhag-ra-tshang. He died in the Iron-Rabbit year of the 15th calendrical cycle (1891) leaving a message (tshems bzhag) that he would be born at Brag-nag-rtsa. During these successors' lives, the rMa-se monastery was kept as the main old Gangkar monastery. The assembly hall and the 6-armed (Mahakala) house became dark, smoky places. The old place was no more, just rundown and dark. A monastic college was not set up.

Then my root teacher, the completely aware and unequalled master[20] Karma bShad-sgrub Chos-kyi Seng-ge arrived and built a new rMa-se monastery from scratch. He started a new monastic college and practice facility. The lamp of the teachings now shined brightly in the gloomy temple of Minyak.

[20] Everywhere the lotus flowers of culture blossomed. The quality of non-sectarianism in spiritual method and the acceptance, without prejudice, of people from many places,[21] was like a goose gliding around on a lake of lotuses. The name of the monastery Khams-gsum-grags (pronounced Kusi-drak) was known everywhere. Generally speaking, my teacher can certainly be counted as the 9th in succession. Following what my most excellent teacher himself maintained, I write of him as the 5th in succession. Nowadays, though the Kham-gsum-grags monastery is the foremost, it gets this position because of the old Bo Gangkar monastery (and the) Gangkar incarnation.

[21] The circumstances of Minyak and special mention of the region of his birth

The fifth in the series of excellent incarnate teachers of Bo Gangkar monastery, Lord Vajradhara, whose qualities are difficult to enumerate, Karma bShad-sgrub Chos-kyi Seng-ge, the banner of his fame in the world gently waving, was born at a place some hundreds of miles to the north of Bodhgaya with nine black mountains, upper reaches covered with snow. This sublime region is at the heart of the world and includes Ti-se and Jo-mo Gangs-dkar, 'Bo Gangs-dkar and rMa-rgyal sBom-ra, surrounded with many peaks looking like pillars in the sky. There are the lakes: mTsho-ma dros-pa,[22] mTsho Khri-shor rGyal-mo, mTsho sKya-ring, Minyak mtsho, Mu-ge tsho, ornamenting the entire region. There are wild yak ('brong), white-muzzled ass (kha-dkar rkyang), blue sheep (gna'-ba), gazelles (rgo-ba) and so forth, herds of wild deer and antelope that look like constellations, roaming about wherever they like. With divine birds, grouse, pheasant, geese, wild ducks, nightingales, and the sweet songs of the cuckoo, everyone feels happy. In the ground there are many hidden treasures: gold, silver, copper, iron, and other [22] mineral deposits; crystals, diamonds and other precious stones. There are open pastures and high plains, forests of white and red pine,[23] and filled with one or more of nine kinds of the world's rhododendrons. In the marshlands and wide valleys where it is not clear where one [valley] ends and another begins, there are big yellow flowers,[24] wormwood,[25] sheep-eye flowers, and mountain-god flowers, beautiful pleasant gardens ('gran-pa). These forests and marshy valleys are filled with various kinds of medicines, cordyceps,[26] ru-rta,[27] rhubarb, whose sweet smells are all-pervasive. The herds of female yak ('bri), yak (g'yag), horses, sheep and other domesticated animals move slowly throughout the region with the herdsmen. People living there enjoy the company of one another, are happy in their work, delight in songs, dancing, games, teasing one another. They are pleasing to look at, skilled in arts, place their confidence in the Buddhist teachings. They oppose what is bad and are skilled in warfare. The place where the warrior people like this live is known throughout the world as Tibet.

As is said:

"Encircled by glaciers like hanging white scarves,
Grass meadows and slate mountains are elephant herds
    posing majestically,
Day and night hold the "earrings" of the sun and moon.
Plants, forests, like a beautiful display of peacock tail
    feathers,
Lakes and ponds, blue skies, like a picture.

[23] Cranes, swans, geese: making music from their throats.
Small meadows: clear mirrors of turquoise,
Wild ass and gazelle, pacing along with the yaks, and
Flocks of sheep in their midst: ornamenting the edges like
    pearls.
Livestock glistening like jeweled stones,
Black yak hair tents spread out on the ground like stars.
Genuinely good people, happy, with complexions glowing in
    joy;
Young women proud in the glory of youth,
Wearing jeweled ornaments and necklaces adorning their
    necks.
Bracelets, shoulder ornaments sound like tinkling bells,
And the mind is absorbed in wonderful joy.

Saffron religious dress: clouds moving over new borders.
Recitation of prayers: the pleasant buzzing of bees.
Sacred teachings: light drizzles of nectar.
The glory of spring is nicer than the realm of the gods!"

So it goes…

Minyak is one of the eight groups of what was once known as the six human tribes[28] in ancient Tibet. In what was called the upper, middle, and lower major areas of Tibet, we have the two regions of Minyak and greater Minyak. These are situated with Mongolians to the North, 'Jang to the South, Chinese to the East, and Tibetans to the West. There is Minyak Gha, the area that was really the original homeland for Minyak, [24] with mDo and sTod Khams in greater Minnyag. There exist a number of words in the old language of Tibet such as *sga* **and** *'ga'*, but since it is a Minyak word it is properly spelled *Gha*.

Generally speaking the kingdom of Minyak came into existence more than 2000 years ago. Although it is certain that there were tens of dynasties, we have not seen any data to make (exact) determinations. I have no confidence in writing something based on assumptions or trust in legends. In China's past, during the fourth dynasty of the Sung,[29] in 1032, the Water-Snake Year, the sixth year of the first calendrical cycle, the capital of the dynasty was taken over by the Minyak King Si-hu.[30] Si-hu is a Minyak word, *Si* having the meaning of "day" and *hu* meaning "night": hence the (one) who is "King, Day and Night", or as the Chinese call the emperor, Trilo. These are words of good wishes for the king, a form of praise.

At the time the motherland, China, to the northeast, had come under the control of the Mongolians and others and even most of mDo and sTod Khams of the 'Jang. The capital of the emperor remained for 195 years. During the ninth dynasty of Minyak kings, rDo-rje dpal, known as Shri-tur in the Mongolian language, lived at the capital Go Thul-ken-han-kan.[31] The Mongolian Pog-ta king, Genghis Khan (Ching-ge-seng), attacked. With great bravery [the Minyak-pa king] stood up to him, blocking him, but at the end, in the Fire-Pig year of the 4th calendrical cycle (1227), he died in the conflict with the invading forces. King rDo-rje dPal's queen was very beautiful in her youth and was known as

Gur-pul cen-go to the Mongolians. Genghis Khan raped her.[32] Risking her life, the queen took revenge for the attack and crushed both of her enemy's testicles.[33] [25] Ching-ge-seng died on the 2nd day of 7th month in that year. The queen committed suicide at Nag-chu.[34] At that point the dynasty of Minyak Gha ended.

At the time of the sixth dynasty of Minyak rGod kings, a minister of the king together with his subjects traveled to gTsang and mNga'-ris and established a base at sTag-sde seng-ge lung.[35] The Minyak lord Lha-btsan legs-pa and his successors stayed there for some generations. Later, after coming down [from sTag], a Minyak leader became a patron of Sa-skya Grags-pa rGyal-mtshan. Over time, as the chief patron of the Sa-skya, he became the ruler of the northern flank. The dynasty of the north is very clearly (mentioned in) the biographies of the Northerner rNam-rgyal Grags-bzang and others. I won't write about it as I am daunted by the amount of writing it would take. If we examine the name rGyal rGod[36] given to the Minyak king in these references, Minyak rGyal rGod is a general term for the dynasty, and clearly not just a name for the last dynasty.

The Minyak word for the Minyak king *Tung-kus* is seen in the Tibetan word *Dar-skud*, where there has been a change in pronunciation since in Minyak *Dar-skud* is pronounced *Tung-kus*. Since China is the source of silk (gos chen) and silk thread (dar skud), this word has this meaning because in the previous dynasty of China silk thread was called "king".[37] *Tong-kun* is a change in pronunciation of *Tung-kus*. The one called the Minyak Tsa-mi rgyal-po also contains Minyak words. *Tsa* is "earth" and *mi* means "sky", hence the meaning of the "master of heaven and earth" or the "King of Heaven and Earth." Even with various combinations of letters in written Tibetan, [26] to depend on keywords in an effort to explain connections to meanings in the language of another people, especially since we cannot know anything for sure, is a fruitless effort.

Even then the royal lineage was scattered, together with subjects, and established bases in Central Tibet (dBus gtsang), Nepal, and India. It is certain that the Bhutanese and Sikkimese kingdoms came from Minyak. The earlier Minyak kingdom had great strength historically and the Minyak people lived in a wide area that included Qinghai, Gansu, and Sichuan. If one were to wonder where they are now, in Qinghai, Gansu and other places there is (for example) the Minyak wing of the monastery at sKu-'bum monastery. One must take into account the fact of many Minyak scholars occupying the highest positions at sKu-'bum and that for a time Qinghai and Gansu had Minyak communities and culture. It is clear that there were many Minyak holy persons. As a result of the conflict between Chinese and Mongolians, Tibetans and Moslems and especially from being beaten down for a long time by the evil Mongolian armies, for the most part the Minyak were changed as a clan by the Mongolian, Hor, Uighur, rGya and Moslem peoples so that even their language fell into disuse. Nowadays, there are still communities scattered about, but in what are called Minyak settlements, the speech is denigrated so that now there are not more than a very small (number of speakers). What happened to the Minyak is like what happened to the Manchu when they were defeated.

[27] In the east of Khams, Minyak ring-mo is between the Nyag and rGyal-mo-dngul rivers. Because of the great distance [from their capital], in the past, the Mongolians could not inflict much harm. Also during the Ming dynasty (1368-1644) the Buddhist teachings flourished. Because of the great kindness of the Five Minyak scholars and others such as Minyak 'Jam-dbyangs Grags-pa, the teachings and study of Minyak culture were wide spread.

At Nyag-rong, rTa'u, mGar-thar,[38] rGyal-rong, Nyag-chu Kha, and rMi-li, there were many Minyak people and Minyak was the main language. Even now in parts of rTa'u and rGyal-rong, Minyak is the main language spoken. As

Dar-rtse-mdo is the "navel" of Khams Minyak, it has not faded away there. From the time of the Ming, it was the capital of the Minyak kingdom. The king was called the lCags-la rGyal-po.[39] Up to now the royal lineage has not been broken and still exists but the lCags-la king's palace is now a ruin.[40] Khams Minyak is a kind of doorway from which learned Tibetans emerged. The Tsa-mi translator Sangs-rgyas grags had gone down to live in India more than 20 years before Atisa went to Tibet. He was an abbot of Nalendra for many years and died in India. The translator Gyi-lJang translated many *sutras* and *tantras* and in particular the teaching cycles of dPal ye-shes-kyi mgon-po. He appreciated all philosophical approaches without distinction. Also many translators and scholars-adepts such as Kva-'od mchog-grags and so forth came from Minyak. Nowadays, there is the Minyak wing at 'Bras-spungs monastery in dBu-tsang, built by people from Khams Minyak. There were the dGal-ldan Khri-pa dam- pa A-mes and kLu-'bum sTong-'dus and so forth, Minyak monks who oversaw the recitation of prayers and the sMon-rams-pa [28] dKon-mchog bsTan-'dzin and others, all people from Khams Minyak.

In the 16th century, at the end of the 10th Tibetan calendrical cycle (1567), the evil armies of the Mongolians headed by the Gushri group attacked the Khams Be-ri[41] kingdom. To direct the attention of Tibetans elsewhere, they attacked the gTsang king. The chief son of Gushri, mKha-'gro bstan-skyong, attacked the 'Jang in Yunnan, coming many times into Minyak and destroying many towns. All the Minyak monasteries were destroyed. The culture that had been built up and cultivated over time disappeared; a gloomy time had come. Even the spoken language changed for the most part. Nowadays those whose primary language is Minyak are not found other than in the Dar-mdo river valley and the Thang-'go community at dGu-rong rdzong.

In early Tibet, during the time of King gLang-dar-ma and the revolt against him in the Earth-Ox year (929), no harm came

27

to the Buddhist teachings in the Minyak region. Teaching of theory and practice spread widely. At that time, at Minyak Gha, the younger bLa-chen dgongs-pa rab-gsal took monk vows with Go-rong seng-ge grags. At Minyak Lha-rtse Bhig-tig he studied wisdom literature and psychology with Ka-'od mchog-grags. In the Minyak region of Khams, many talented Minyak students of the translators (Lotsawa) Tsa-mi and sMri-ti came from the areas of 'Dan and thereabouts. Specifically, at the monasteries in the east of Khams at Minyak ring-mo, from the previous Mongolian to the Ming period, explanation, study, meditation, and practice for the many monks greatly increased. During the 17th century, at the beginning of the Manchu dynasty, [29] Mongolian armies demolished the monasteries and killed most of the monks. The teachings diminished and even those who knew the culture disappeared.

Circumstances of his birth and younger years

In the former Mongolian period, most of the territory of Tibet was known as districts like those in the three upper jurisdictions of rNga', the middle four provinces or parts of dBu-gtsang, and the six ridges of mDo Khams, famous like the wind. The best and highest of the ridges which would become the most important is Minyak rab-sgang.[42] Here the Tibetan king Srong-btsan sgam-po[43] built the last of 108 temples, bordering China at the eastern gate. Since the temple was built there, it was called Rab-stong tshar-sgang. It is a joy to look at the rich earth stretching out like a single piece of white silk over an area from the Northwest to the Southeast between the Minyak nyag-chu and rGyal-mo dngul chu[44] (Yuan jiang). This location in an area east of the central part of Tibet is known as Shar (Eastern) Minyak rong-mo. In the center of the upper part where high pastures meet the cultivated fields (rTsva-chu), in this space of cultivated and high-pasturage land where cereal and dairy production blend, there is an area farmed at a lower altitude where five different grains and different varieties of trees grow. The climate is balanced, neither too hot or too cold, supporting a comfortable life style. People are good-natured and honest,[45] [31] kind to the weak and courageous in defying those who are bad. Matters of jurisdiction and other agreements are bound by oaths. People help each other, delight in dancing and public amusements and place their trust in the Buddhist teachings.

In a place where cultivated and open pasturage over lap ('dres-ma), what is nowadays called Sa-sde-chus, there was a solitary dwelling, the best in the area, imbued with the ten virtues of a place.[46] At the house called Gil-ti Brag-nag tshang, on the morning of the 15 day of 9th month, in the Water-Female-Snake year of the 15th calendrical cycle (1893), just as the sun was shining on the mountain peaks, a son was born to the father Brag-nag 'phrin-las, and mother Brag-nag sgrol-ma. He was said to be a new Lotus Incarnation. The night before a light snow had fallen, and in the area around Bo Gangkar monastery, tiger tracks were clearly visible in the snow. Ravens and magpies called out from the roof of the house. Dharma guardians of the Oral Transmission (bKa'-brgyud-pa) and the gods, together with a retinue of vultures floating about in the sky, came in welcome and were seen as wondrous omens.

The little boy stayed at home with his parents for a few years and developed much more rapidly than others in strength and intelligence. Many signs of accomplishment were visible, impressions of his foot and hands left on rocks. You can still see them, even now.

"...impressions of his foot and hands left on rocks.
You can still see them."

When he was three, following the last will and testament of his predecessor, the 15th Karmapa, all-knowing master mKha'- khyab rdo-rje, while at Lhasa from sTod-lung mTshur-phu, the great seat of the rGyal-ba'i dbang-po Karmapas, confirmed [the rebirth] through a "seeing" arising from original awareness.

Gil-ti Brag-nag tshang, Gangkar Rinpoche's birthplace at Sa-sde-chus

[32] He issued a statement that the region of the birth, characteristics of the house including the parents, was very clearly indicated as he wrote in his letter. At the monastery, elders who were not knowledgeable (in these aspects) of the custom (of recognizing incarnations) did not dare decide by themselves. They commissioned two monks, 'Byor-dbus phun-tshogs and 'Khor-sa bsTan-'phel, to take the prophesy letter and go to dPal-spungs to seek the advice of Si-tu Rinpoche Padma dbang-mchog rgyal-po. When they had fully understood the meaning of the letter and had a direct understanding of the prophecy, the two monks returned to the monastery. Right away, with the permission of the monastery and the incarnation from 'Ge-ba monastery, a group consisting of a servant from the King at lCags and some monks, took the hat, drum and ritual instruments and a

second item like [the original] that belonged to the previous lineage holder, Karma Tshe-ring dbang-po, and went to Brag-nag tshang. After [the child correctly] identified [the right items], complete trust arose and they invited the Precious Incarnation to the monastery. All patrons and priest monks felt boundless joy that the favorable circumstances of his enthronement were completed in their entirety. Then, following discussion amongst all the senior and younger monks, bLa-ma nor-bu as he was called, of the nomad Rig-'dzin clan, knowing rites (cho ga), ritual practice (phyag len), melodies and tunes in ritual music, recipient of many empowerments, literary and ritual permissions, and respected as a monk of good character, was appointed his reading tutor.

When the Precious Incarnation was five,[47] in the year of the Fire-Chicken of the 15th calendrical cycle (1897), he was made the head of the reading students. At that time at Khams-gsum-grags monastery there was nothing apart from an old assembly hall and protectors' house in disrepair. There was no place to stay.

[33] For a long time, life at the old Gangkar monastery had not been happy. Near Khams-gsum-grags monastery, at a juncture in the rMu-rgyu valley, is a small village known as Sog-po. He established his residence there at a small temple [built by] Thang-stong rgyal- po and continued his studies. A few monks lived there with the Precious Incarnation. Monks had gathered there at the Thang-rgyal temple for many years for the fasting and silent observances on the anniversary of the (Buddha's) Awakening. One evening when he was seven, during a very subtle moment, a deep awareness came forth by itself and he spontaneously composed a prayer in verse to master Padmasambhava. His teacher Norbu was amazed by his wisdom (mkhyen rab). Developing even more confidence[48] as he did so, Rinpoche continuously prayed and performed *puja* (made offerings). Little by little he practiced until reaching competency in the three: reading, calligraphy, and composition; playing horns, drums and preparation and

32

music, singing and dancing. He trained without hindrance in all disciplines (rigs), chiefly in the Kagyu text <u>Chos-spyod rab-gsal</u>. He memorized the twelve great rites, the mandala rituals including Kun-rig, 'Phag-mo dgu-gtor and the five great collections of prayers.[49] He listened to many stories and anecdotes told by the elder monks who were his attendants, (such as) the time the adept Thang-stong rgyal-po came to the town of Sog-po, and because of the deceit of the herdsmen, displayed many kinds of magical powers. He developed more and more confidence in earlier adepts of the Kagyu-pa.

Zhag-ra tshang, the dwelling where the previous incarnation Karma Tshe-ring dBang-po was born, was very near the village of Sog-po. Every time the young boy went to the offering house at Zhag-ra tshang where the previous incarnation used to stay, he would say that the shrine objects, robes, and images "are mine, yet some are not." One time when he said "are not" a direct perception came about, a recollection of memories from his previous life.

The wish arose to go study and train at a monastery where there were educated individuals, both learned and accomplished. [34] His teacher Lama Norbu said; "I do not know more than ritual observances and methods used in the monastery. I can't fulfill Rinpoche's wishes and I have reached the limit of what I know. Now it would be better if you went to a bigger place where you can learn more."

Then, after discussions with the officials of the monastery and in agreement with the wishes of both the Precious Incarnation and his teacher Norbu, it was decided that he would go to Dege Palpung (sDe-dge dpal-spungs). The previous incarnation had gone to the monastery there and had been a student of Si-tu Pad-ma Nyin-byed dBang-po.

Like a white lotus in the center of a lotus garden and
      the moon amid stars and planets,
The wisest man among many wise men,
      In this whole world, was born as its adornment.

Thang-rgyal temple (photo Minyak Gonpo)

[35] Entering the spiritual life and through efforts in study and contemplation attaining a state of learning

In the Iron-Dog Year (1910) of the 15th calendrical cycle, when he was 15, he set out for the great monastic seat at Khams sDe-dge dPal-spungs. On the way he went to see mGar-thar[50] monastery where the 7th Dalai Lama bskal-bzang rgya-mtsho had stayed for some time, and rTa'u Nya-mtsho and Hor Brag-'go[51] monasteries. He met all the incarnate lamas at each monastery. Then, after visiting the dKar-mdzes sDe monastery, he went to the Ban-gran monastery at Rong-pa-tsha. There a new seat had been built for the Gyalwang Karmapa and he looked at the many marvelous indications of accomplishment at the Lord Karmapa Dus-gsum mKhyen-pa's birthplace. Generally speaking dKar-mdzes is a place where many adepts, Kagyupa teachers, incarnations of the Karmapas and the Sharmapas such as Chos-grags Ye-shes and so on, have been born. Although there were many adepts to meet, again he set out; once more he was busy with his journey. He visited the temple at sDe-dge of Thang-stong rGyal-po, the practice cave, and great monastery of Lhun-grub-steng.[52] Then he arrived at the main monastery of dPal-spungs which is not far from there.

[36] Because of the fame of its scholars, dPal-spungs has been well known since the 17th century, or the 11th Tibetan calendrical cycle, throughout India, China, dBu-tsang and Khams. The translator, great Pandita, Kun-mkhyen Chos-kyi 'byung-gnas started it soon after he came there.[53] It has become the center for all Tibetan culture: grammar, poetics, construction[54] and healing arts, language and rhetoric.[55] There were not only the great scholars of Khams such as Tshe-dbang kun-khyab, mChog-sprul bsTan-'dzin Chos-kyi Nyi-ma, dBon Nges-legs and so on, but their close disciples, Kon-sprul Yon-tan rgya-mtsho, 'Ju Mi-pham, rDzogs-chen dPal-sprul and their students as well. There were lineages of instruction based on the practices (rig gnas) in the mDo, sMad, and bLa-brang parts of the monastery, though all these evolved from the dPal-spungs instruction lineage. Because of that, it was a place where all would gather, [coming] from countries everywhere to train in Tibetan culture. The teachings on scriptural transmission, direct experience, explication and practice spread. sDe-dge dPal-spung was like a gateway from which learned and accomplished individuals emerged.[56]

When the Precious Teacher arrived at dPal-spungs, right away he met Si-tu Padma dBang-mchog rGyal-po, dPon-rgan Rin-po-che, and the great scholars Tshe-dbang dPal-'byor and bDe-chen Nges-don bsTan-'dzin Rab-rgyas. Situ Rinpoche was overjoyed and gave him the scriptural authorization (lung) for writing the six-lettered *mani*.[57] Si-tu said: "'Bo-sprul, you have developed good qualities and must study hard to become a scholar and an adept." Those who came to dPal-spungs from Gangs (dkar) monastery were called 'Bo-pa. As an incarnated lama (*sprul-sku*) he was called 'Bo-sprul ("Mountain Incarnation"). *'Bo* is a Minyak language word for mountain.

[37] First, since ethics and manners are the basis and ground for all knowledge, he went before the great scholar/abbot (mKhan-chen) Ka-rma bDe-chen Nges-don bsTan-'dzin rab-rgyas. He took the vows of a first-year layman renunciate

which are also those of a novice monk. All that was to be observed in regard to the vows he guarded like his eyes. On many days he slept without loosening his belt. He studied the writings of teacher kLu-sgrub (Nagajuna) with the scholar Tshe-dbang dpPal-'byor. Stopping at chapter 15, he reached the middle of his study of the commentary on the monastic code.[58] Then, with the abbot of the scriptural center (bshad grva), gZhan-dga' Rin-po-che, he studied the 13 great commentaries on the sutras and the root Sutra/Monastic Code, The Sayings of Arya-Gunaprabha,[59] the two disciplinary code texts of the Sutra on Individual Liberation,[60] the writings of professor dByig-gnyen (Vasubandhu), the Treasure of Phenomenology (*Abhidharmakosa*),[61] the two commentaries on the Collection of Abridged Texts of the *Abhidharma*[62] by the exalted Thogs-med (Arya-Asanga); four commentaries on the view: the Root Discriminative-Appreciation[63] text of kLu-sgrub (Nagajuna); On the Entrance to the Central View[64] by Zla-ba grags pa (Candrakirti); A Treatise on the Central View in 100 Verses by 'Phags-pa'i lha (Aryadeva),[65] and Entering into the Conduct of a *Bodhisattva*[66] by Zhi-ba-lha (Santideva). With the five treatises, The Jewel of Complete Realized Understanding of Discriminative Appreciation,[67] A Jewel of *Sutras*,[68] On the Distinction Between the Central and the Extremes,[69] On the Nature of Things in Themselves,[70] The Highest *Tantra*[71] and the book by the exalted Thogs-med (Arya Asanga) known as the Questions Made in Public to the Venerable Maitreya at the *Akanishta* Heavens[72] he completed the core of his education. By the time he had spent two years at the scriptural college his teacher gZhan-phan Rinpoche was extremely pleased with his creative and discerning intellect. Before many scholars he praised him by saying:

"If one looks at this discriminative appreciation which you have developed, it is certainly like that of Chos-rje Sa-pan and Kun-mkhyen kLong-chen-pa."[38]

When he was 21, he went before the abbot Karma bDe-chen nges-don bsTan-'dzin rab- rgyas, who had previously given him his novice monk's vows, and received the complete vows of a monk. The name, Ka-rma bShad-sgrub Chos-kyi Seng-ge, given to him before when he was recognized by Karmapa mKha'-khyab rDo-rje, was not changed. Continuing where he left off, he listened to and thought about a veritable ocean of doctrines on the *sutras* and *tantras*. With lNga-rig sMra-ba'i Pan-chen bKra-'phel and mKhas-grub Kun-gyi Khyu-mchog, mKhan-chen Tshe-dbang dPal-'byor and others he studied the cycle of ordinary subjects - grammar, poetics, astrology, medicine, rhetoric, fabrication technique - studying these properly, completing all, even the synopses and introductions. Then he went on a religious pilgrimage to sacred places in dBu-tsang, visiting Se-ra, 'Bras-spungs, dGa'-ldan, and bSam-yas. He made offerings and recited prayers in ceremonies at sacred places, the Jo (khang), and Sha-ka.[73] Especially, after he arrived at the great seat and source of the Practice Lineage teachings, sTod-lung mTshur-phu, he requested, mostly from master rGyal-dbang Karma-pa mKha'-khyab rdo-rje, the deep teachings of the Kagyupa; the path of technique: Six Doctrines of Naropa; the path of liberation: the scriptural transmission and instructions on Clear Light ('od-gsal) and phyag-chen (*Mahamudra*) ; the processes of development and simultaneous connection with Vajrayogini; process of perfection: the explanations and instructions on the inseparability of mind and the vital force,[74] the Guhyasamaja teachings according to the lineage from the translator Marpa; the common instructions and all-encompassing empowerments in the cycle of the incomparable tantras of 'Khor-lo bde-mchog (*Cakrasamvara)*, rDo-rje gdan-gzhi and so on. Not long after returning to dPal spungs, [39] with 'Jam-mgon Si-tu Pad-ma dBang-mchog rGyal-po, Grub-dbang dPon-rgan Rin-po-che, gNas-lnga Rig-pa'i Pandita rDo-rje 'Dzin-dbang Mangala Dharma Wardha, mKhan-chen gZhan-dga' Rin-po-che, the sun of the earlier translation teachings. and other previous teachers and a dozen or so spiritual friends, he studied the deep teachings of the Ka-rma bka'-brgyud, Jo-nang bka'-brgyud,[75] Shangs-pa bka'-brgyud, the "secret mantra" (i.e. tantric)(gSang-sngags) teaching of the Nyingmapa in the seven treasures, the "Three Cycles on Easing the Mind" (Ngal-gso skor gsum), "Mother-Son Heart Teachings" (sNying-thig ma-bu), "Wisdom Teacher Instructions" (Khrid Ye-shes bla-ma)[76] and other deep instructions of the rDzogs-chen on the clear light, the ultimate "state" of the nine vehicles.[77] He was made abbot for the summer retreat where he taught and gave empowerments for a year. At those times 'Jam-mgon Si-tu Pad-ma dbang-mchog made him his very close disciple[78] and appointed him the foremost among his attendants (mgron gnyer). Encouraged to write by 'Jam-mgon Situ and mKhan-chen gZhan-phan Rin-po-che, he wrote many works that pleased the scholars such as the Commentary on the Special Praises to the Exalted One,[79] Questions and answers arranged as 21 questions by the scholar Karma Nges-don from eastern rGyal mo rong,[80] the sPyod-'jug commentary 'Phror lus, and a critical analysis of *Madyamika* and *prajnaparamita*. Conditions didn't come together and they didn't carve the blocks for the Commentary on the Special Praises to the Exalted One at dPal-pungs so there's nothing at the printing house.

At dPal lhun-grub, a monastery above the main one, when the sDe-dge Sa-skyong ("Earth Protector') became the ruler, he gave useful advice imbued with five qualities.[81] The five spiritual advisors of sDe-dge,[82] among many chiefs, and [40] the scholars and reincarnates were all delighted, scattered flowers in praise and respect in every direction. Although he was young, everyone was amazed at his scholarly attainments and confidence. He made a pilgrimage to all the monasteries in the group of sDe-dge monasteries: Ka:thog monastery, established by the Ka-dam-pa bde-shegs; rDzogs-chen monastery, founded by the rDzogs-chen Padma Rigs-'dzin; "Great Monastery",[83] famous for having been established by Thang-stong rgyal-po. Senior, junior monks and benefactors at each monastery were all very happy to see him. He had many debates on doctrines and held discussions on spiritual practice with scholars wherever they lived. Gradually the fame of his scholarship spread throughout the three (areas) of dBu, Tsang and Khams. When he was 25, he was made the combined retreat teacher and practice master for a 3 year, 3 month retreat at the dPal-spungs retreat house. By using a teaching style using few words, he summarized the main points of the instructions on the cycle of physical training (lus sbyong), the stabilization (gnas) (of the energy) in the pathways, the breath as vital energy, and vitalizing energy as the result. These practices were easy to understand. He added additional gems (of instruction) from the main techniques of the Shangs-pa bka'-brgyud pa about removing obstacles through stopping the breath, grasping the energizing forces (thig-le) and recognizing the formative energetic configurations (thig-le), methods from Virupa in the Sa-skya-pa and rDzogs-chen from the Nyingmapa.. Because concepts were explained gradually and presented in an easy to understand way, his companions and fellow practice masters were completely satisfied in their understanding. A retreat master such as he, having qualities of both understanding and realization, had never been seen [at the monastery] except for one or two others.

Students of the abbot, gZhan-dga' Rin-po-che, at that time were very skilled. For example, [41] although there were scholars such as Zur-mang[84] mChog-sprul Pad-rnam and Tsha-tsha mkhan-po Thub-bstan, dBon-stod mKhyen-rab, sTobs-bcu Rab-rgyas and so forth, the foremost of all those in the study centers were bLa-ma Rin-po-che 'Bo-sprul and Zur-mang Pad-rnam. Due to an insatiable thirst for the nectar of sacred non-sectarian teachings and philosophies in the twelve years he stayed at sDe-dge dPal-spungs, he had become deeply accomplished in understanding reality as it is and as it appears.

Like a captain steering a boat filled with treasures back home, when he was thirty, in the Water Dog Year of the 15th calendrical cycle (1922) and feeling very happy, he went back to his own monastery in Minyak. Separated for a long time from his mother and father by all his studies and spiritual practice, they met as if for the first time. Joy and confidence spread spontaneously; smiling, unable to hold back their tears, they welcomed him back from far away to his monastery, Khams-gsum-grags.

In a place where people consider one
Who pretends to be learned to be the shining sun because a firefly appears,
For the sake of beings there shines one of brilliance in scripture and logic.

[42] Nourished by a foundation in the Buddhist teachings, spreading his learning out slowly and uniformly in all directions

When he came down from sDe-dge he was now a senior monk. 'Byor-dbus Phun-tshogs sDe-lnga bDe-legs, sDe-lnga Rig-grol, A-khva Thub-bstan, dPal 'byor A-bu and others were appointed as his advisors. Phag dbu-thar A-'bum was appointed treasurer (phyag-mdzod) together with Dam-pa mkhyen-rab as his attendant (gsol-dpon). He started the restoration of the assembly hall of rMa-se monastery. This work was carried out by the stone masons rDo-rje mgon-po and Legs-dbu bSod-nams don-grub. All senior and junior monks of the monastery made immense efforts. Help was provided later without pretext and with utmost sincerity by the ordinary people and benefactors of the area. The assembly hall was successfully completed with four layers and 16 pillars. Then, over many years of effort, additions were made: a summer retreat house (dbyar gnas khang), an Urgyan temple, a sku gdung temple,[85] and a protector temple[86] (mgon khang). Stones were laid down flat in an area that could hold a thousand people and surrounding this in three layers were monks' homes on the perimeter, the home (gzim shag) of the teacher and the winter and summer residences, together with many more homes of monks, caretakers, and one for the treasurer of the monastic household (bla-brang).

[43] Many carpenters were invited from Chung la'i[87] Sichuan, and they built the assembly hall with a Chinese roof and most excellent pedestals for the monastery gods, offerings, books and so forth. Image makers (lha bzo ba) from rTa'u rGyal-'phags[88] monastery and designers (lha ris-pa) from rGyal-mo-rong rNam-rgyal[89] monastery, together with wood carvers from Cha-phreng,[90] were invited many times. All the images inside and outside the monastery were finished. After that, traveling over time to dBu lha-ldan on two occasions and to China three times, students and benefactors made many devotional offerings that became an unimaginable support.[91]

These were three images[92] of gold and silver as inner symbols for the monastery, various kinds of gems which did not have a market price, gold seals of the upper and lower (branches), offerings of silk fabric (gos chen), various ritual instruments made from gold, silver, brass, copper or bronze. For example, there were nearly 2000 gold images of varying sizes. In its role as the monastic seat and mother monastery of all those in Minyak, there were more offerings though it wasn't the largest (monastery).   It became a place where groups from monasteries that took part in the non-sectarian philosophical movement in Khams found their needs met. After the foundation had been finished, rMa-se monastery could complete construction work. The monastery on O-rong-shis Phag-mo Mountain in the series of monasteries at Nyag-chu was kept going. Offerings were also made of dancing costumes and masks. Summer groups (retreats) started up again. At dGu-rong, Shar-kha Rong-grub-pa monastery was built from the ground up. The appointees, bLa-bsko Tshul-khrims Phun-tshogs and Tshe-dbang rGyal-mtshan, were commissioned as before. Having taken the offering practices on by himself at the mTsho-zhabs U-rgyan temple,[93] g'Yang-'khod bLa-ma bSod-nams was appointed master of the monastery. A series of newly established monasteries started with a new monastery in the area of dGu-rong ta-khog. [44] bLa-ma Yon-tan rGya-mtsho, bsTan-pa Rab-rgyas, 'Jang-bla Shes-rab, and dBang- tshogs Tshul-khrims were appointed monastery masters as before. The number of monks grew. Having established a monastery as a forest retreat at the grey-slate rock on the upper slopes above the middle of the mountain at lCang-'gram beyond Nyag-chu-kha, Yon-tan rGya-mtsho was made the master of that monastery. 'Brog-sprul brTson-'grus mThar-phyin[94] was made the teacher after he established the sDig-dag monastery at Shar-ri beyond gNas-chen pho-brang lnga-rtse.[95] After the Go-Tshang-'og monastery had been built in the village of Nyi-'od-zhod beyond Nyag-chu-kha, Ngag-dbang Chos-grags was appointed as the teacher. Again the monastery appointed gZhi- ring 'Jang-bla Zla-ba as monastery leader since he had built a series of more than ten monasteries beyond Nyag chu kha. A new ground for the Buddha's teachings was established. The Kagyupa monasteries beyond Nyag in upper and lower Minyak that had become rundown were restored and those that weren't in need of repair were improved. The bKa'-brgyud teachings became like the sunrise.

Rinpoche returned to his homeland and spent more than two years in meditation (bsnyen sgrub) not far away at Gangs-dkar Byams-sa[96] mountain retreat. He taught the "Inner Sciences" (Nang-don rig-pa) and "Grammar and Poetry" (Sum-rtags snyan-ngag) to the head cook bLa-ma mkhyen-rab and a few students such as Tshul-khrims Zla-ba. He practiced the ritual visualization (sadhana) of bDe-mchog, rGyal-ba rgya-mtsho, sGrol-dkar (White Tara), sPyan-ras-gzigs (Chenrezik) and so forth. Signs and indications beyond imagining came in dreams and (meditation) experience. Below the retreat house (imprints of) the hands and feet of mGon-po nag-po appeared by themselves. Places appeared where there were many indications of realization. Since there is a tradition that these were kept very secret by the lama, I dare not write about these many spots.

[45] Tshul-khrims Zla-ba, as the most outstanding Minyak student, tutored many Tibetan language students from 'Ba'-thang[97] and foreign countries.[98] He was a teacher of Tibetan literature for ten years at the Central Minorities University (Krung dbyangs mi rigs slob grva) and trained many literary Tibetan specialists (bod-yig mkhan-pa). Rinpoche, seeing that some of his students had such capabilities, was very pleased and encouraged them with praise and compliments. For example, these remarks were written down of what was said to Tshul-khrims zla-ba at the monastery: "Tshul khrims, your intellect is a stainless full moon enveloped with a thousand cool rays of light. All benefits for others happen the moment it emerges form the ocean depths; oh, may the mountain-side of dharma teachings quickly come here!" It is clear if one looks at the words.

In the Fire Tiger year of the 15th calendrical cycle when he was 34 (1925) the Minyak Ri-khud monastery[99] incarnation invited Rinpoche to his monastery. At Ri-khud monastery, a new school was established. He taught the study of the five arts and sciences for three years. The students' understanding and disciple greatly increased. A new summer retreat was built and he was the chief abbot. He gave layman, *bodhisattva* and *vajrayana* vows to many people. He gave many empowerments, scriptural authority, ritual permissions to the Ri-khud mchog-sprul and his nephew, who was an incarnation, and monks, workers, officials of the monastery. On many occasions he gave religious empowerments in marketplaces (khrom dbang). Although this Ri-khud monastery is the main Minyak Sa-skya monastery, its circumstances were modest. After the decline of Minyak, this school [46] was the first one built that met the standards for a school. Many scholars arrived and stayed over a 30-year period. The [Buddhist] teachings grew, education increased and great benefit came about.

Kusi drak (Khams-gsum-grags) monastery
(photo: Minyag Gonpo)

In the Iron Dragon year of the 16th calendrical cycle (1940) when Rinpoche was 48, at his own monastery, Khams-gsum-grags, he established a new school at Byams-chen Chos-'khor gLing to teach all aspects of culture (rig gnas) together. To each student every month Rinpoche gave thirty pounds[100] of grain and some cash, butter and tea twice each day, plus allowances for all spiritual gatherings (chos tshogs) and religious festivals (dus chen). As for medicine, Rinpoche gave it out whenever it was needed.

Rinpoche himself was the chief teacher and abbot. The younger abbot was Karma Phan-bde bKra-shis, the lead chanter Grags-pa don-yod, and the monitor of conduct A-wa chos-grags. At first, of about 40 students, there were Tibetans, Chinese and 'Jang (from Yunnan). There were dGe-shes and incarnate lamas from the Sa-skya, dGe-lugs, bKa'-brgyud, and Nyingmapa. After more than 2 years had passed at the school, he invited mKhan-po Thub-bstan from sDe-dge. [The mKhan-po] stayed for four years teaching the 30 great commentaries in the cycle of *sutras, tantras*, Hevajra (tantra), and once again the collected writings of Byang-chub dPal along with his mid-length work on poetry. Discipline at the monastery was improved as well as efforts at maintaining it. mKhan-po Thub-bstan spoke kindly to his students. His character was marked by his total commitment to a habit of monastic discipline. He never neglected his students. [47]

During that time Rinpoche gave many deep instructions[101] to Buddhist laymen who came from each region of China and Tibet, Chinese monks (hva-shang), spiritual friends in the non-sectarian philosophical movement (ris-med) and high reincarnations. These instructions included the Hevajra, Kalacakra, instructions on the Guhyasamaja, root and commentary on the "Profound Inner Meaning" (Zab-mo nang-gi don), the nonduality of mind and vital energy, *Mahamudra,* Ocean of Ultimate Meaning and the "Wisdom Teacher Instructions" (Khrid ye-shes bla-ma.[102] When he wasn't teaching he gave many empowerments, scriptural transmissions and permissions. To the students at the college he offered not only his own instructions on grammar, the Root Grammar in Thirty Verses, medicine, astrology, poetry (snyan ngag) and rhetoric, but he also taught his discourses on epistemology, clapping and other gestures of the body, gestures of speech (such as) uttering "dhi skad" (during debate), and how to do the dances like at dGa (ldan), 'Bras (dpungs), Ser (ra) in central (Tibet). Later he went to the monasteries of the dGe-lugs, Nyingmapa, and Sa-skya-pa in upper Min-nyag: sKabs-'gar lha-sgang, Brag-mkhar, Ba-ri, Seng-ge, sKyid-gling[103] and so forth. He gave the sKyid-gling sprul-sku Chos-kyi rGya-mtsho, Brag-mKhar sPrul-sku Pad-rdor, Brag-mkhar sPrul-sku Kun-bzang and the Ba-[104]gnas sPrul-sku much instruction and profound teachings on *vajrayana*. Specifically, many times he gave the deep teachings (khrid) on the Matrix of Mystery cycle of teachings of the Nyingmapa *vajrayana*, the seven treasures of kLong-chen-pa,[105] "Three Cycles of Easing the Mind" (Ngal gso skor gsum), "Mother-Son Heart Teachings (sNying-thig ma-bu), "Wisdom Teacher Instructions" (Khrid ye-shes bla–ma) and the deepest instructions on rDzogs-chen, the sheer lucency ('od gsal) which is the peak of the nine pathways. Blending the two streams of the highest possible state from the Kadampa and *mahamudra* traditions, he presented in an authentic way what one could really rely on in the synthesis of bKa'-(brgyud) and rNying-(ma) teachings. The master of the glorious Sa-skya-pa, the incarnation of Gha thar-lam[106] monastery, [48] most excellent bsTan-pa'i Nyi-ma[107] came quite some distance to be with Rinpoche. Together we attended lectures on grammar, the Root Grammar in Thirty Verses (sum rtags) and poetry. When the 'Jang-bLa sGrol-dkar sPrul-sku[108] arrived there together with his retinue, he stayed on at the school for a year teaching the (Buddhist) sciences. Since there were many Han students studying at the school, it was not possible for all to ask questions. The main person to handle questions was the second son of the Qongqing mayor,[109] Zhang Chen

47

Qi, who, by 1946, had been there for six years. Through tremendous discipline he became very learned. He later went to India, spent some time in retreat there and then went to America. There he became a great professor at university. He translated many deep teachings of the Kagyupa into English such as the Biography and Hundred Thousand Songs of Milarepa. On previous occasions during offering ceremonies at the monastery such as the Great Prayer Festival and so forth he left sacred images. Later, when the monastery was being repaired he offered assistance and showed much kindness to the monastery. In America, he had quite a few students. He has now died.

Chen Qi Po was much disciplined, very knowledgeable in *vajrayana*, and spent some years in retreat engaging in spiritual practice. He translated the Biography of Milarepa into Chinese. He understood the written language of many countries. He lived in Chengdu for a long time before he died.

Chen Ja Ming studied with Rinpoche for some time. Although he was not skilled in reading Tibetan texts, he was very clever in writing, composing texts in Chinese. He dwelt for a long time in retreat in holy places in India. He wrote many Chinese books based on the cycle of teachings of the Kagyupa. He has now died.[110]

The lay woman Hu Yao Long was from Jiangsu. She was the daughter of a great professor from Yunnan University. [49] She stayed with Rinpoche for a long time. She became very skilled in spoken and written Tibetan and served as Rinpoche's interpreter.[111] From 1952 onwards she was weighed down by obstacles. Later, she started writing a few unedited sections of a biography of Rinpoche in Chinese, but died soon after.

Even now, the Jiangxi Chinese monk (Hva shang) Man Kong who spoke little, was very disciplined with deep understanding and experience, is well-known as the master of the Jiangxi main monastery (dgon chen). It is said that he still lives there nowadays.

Earlier, Rinpoche had another translator, a monk named Man khung from Chongqing. His spoken Tibetan was very good but he was not as skilled in translating into Chinese. His basic character was very good and he stayed with Rinpoche for a long time. Now he has passed away I hear.[112]

Other than the Chongqing benefactors and monks (hva shang) and monks who came from Chengdu and Ya'an,[113] there were many lay people who came from Shanghai, Guangdong[114] and so on. If one were to write of all of them it would be too much, so this is just a brief mention of them. In the summer retreat[115] and during the winter season[116] there were many students who studied for a short time, coming from the monasteries in upper Minyak. For example there was Lho-ri Lhag-pa from Ri-khud monastery, Rig-rdor and Rin-grags from Bar-ri[117] monastery, bSod-nam sByin-pa and Nges-don bsTan-'dzin from Lha-sgang[118] monastery and so on like this. And Nam-mkha'i Nor-bu who is now in Italy, great professors from the Central Minorities University (Krung dbyan Mi rigs slob grva chen po) including Tong Jin Hua, Wang Yao, Geng Yu Fang, sKal bzang 'gyur med, Huang Bu Fan[119] and so forth, practicing for as much as a year at Gangs-dkar monastery. [50]
Later (Huang Bu Fan) invited Rinpoche to Beijing where he stayed for three years at the Central Minorities University.[120] Well known in Chinese and Tibetan research were the senior professors Yu Dao Quan,[121] Zhang Yi Sun,[122] Li An Zhai,[123] Wang Yi Nuan,[124] Liu Li Qian[125] and so forth, all of them studying (with Rinpoche) for sure, but it is not clear for how long. In short, Rinpoche worked to increase teachings of the *sutras* and *tantras* of Tibet in Chinese, and to expand the development of research into Chinese and Tibetan studies. This work is not finished.

In the Water-Sheep Year of the 16th calendrical cycle (1943), during the 10th Tibetan month, having reached rGer on the shores of the Nyag-chu, he settled a dispute that had been going on for some time, as follows:

"In the Ta-khog region on the shores of the Nyag-chu:
Households of both Tshe-ring phun-tshogs and A-lab, and
Their kinsmen across the Nyag-chu,
Because of disputes incited by each, returned anger for anger.
Accustomed to this for a long time,
Back and forth more than 70 people, one for one,
Came to lose life so dear.
The moment he saw that sorrowful, anguished-filled place where each destroyed the other and lessened their own circumstances,
Not able to bear this in his compassion, together with his
            retinue, [51]
He arrived at that place to settle the dispute.
For both parties, back and forth, he made the Buddhist teachings come down like nectar.
To the faithful, eyes filling with tears, he said:
"From now on stick to this:
"Do not do evil deeds."
Repeating these words, promising to do this,
They brought their hands together over their heads,
Bowing again and again to his feet."

Traveling on two occasions to dBu-lha-ldan for the enthronement (on the golden throne) of the Gyalwang Karmapa mchog-sprul and to be his mentor

When he was 38 in 1930 in the Iron Horse Year of the 16th calendrical cycle, Rinpoche installed the 16th Karmapa Rig-pa'i rdo-rje on the golden throne. To be the tutor for the Karmapa, he traveled twice to dBu-lha-ldan by horse. Crossing the Nyag-chu, he (took) the southern route to Lithang and Chamdo (Chab-mdo), stopping to meet practitioners at most monasteries he came to along the route. In particular he gave empowerments and ritual permissions at the monasteries belonging to the Karmapa at gNas-nang and so on. He energetically gave spiritual teachings, including empowerments, to people in the marketplaces, expounding the doctrine of giving up evil activity and practicing what is wholesome, adding the scriptural authority for the six syllables.

Before coming to Lithang a Minyag robber showed up and at 'Gas-rba'u-rong some of Rinpoche's things were handed over to the robber to carry. When Rinpoche had finished his dedication prayers, in an awareness state in which distinctions between the action, doer and object did not pertain, he told the bandit: "I cannot take my things back. From now on, stop being a robber." And saying this, he did not take his things back.

Three months passed. Then, after arriving at sTod-rlung mTshur-phu in dBus, seat of the Gyalwang Karmapa, he met the Karmapa himself,[126] [53] the great father of Lord Karmapa, the great dakini of the former Karmapa,[127] gNas-nang dPa'-bo Rinpoche, rGyal-tshab Rin-po-che and so forth, all the officials who had come to the monastic seat. The Tshur-phu monastery lamas and benefactors made a great joyous welcome. When the 16th Karmapa was enthroned on the golden throne, at a great teaching Rinpoche spoke about the main monastery, the expanded *mandala*, and gave excellent advice of five most excellent qualities. There were a lot of smiling, happy faces among the thousand scholars, (much) cheering and scattering of flowers in praise. Following an earnest request from the teachers and benefactors at Tshur-phu and with the encouragement of Si-tu Pad-ma dbang-mchog rgyal-po, Rinpoche stayed for more than a year as tutor for the Karmapa. Rinpoche provided a basic education for the Karmapa. He gave gNas-nang dPa'-bo Rin-po-che, rGyal-tshab Rin-po-che, and Kagyupa incarnate teachers empowerments, scriptural authorizations, permissions and instructions. He also provided many detailed explanations on deep spiritual teachings of the Kagyupa such as bDe-mchog (*Cakrasamvara*), *Mahamaya*, rDo–rje gdan-bzhi, principle *tantra*s, phyag-chen (*mahamudra*) , six doctrines of Naropa, and the Bka'-gdams "Seven Points of Mind Training" (bLo-sbyong don-bdun). He gave empowerments and scriptural authorization many times to the spiritual communities at Tshur-phu and gNas-nang monasteries. He went on spiritual pilgrimage to the three monasteries near Lha-sa: Se-ra, 'Bras-spung, dGa'-ldan. He debated several dGe-lugs-pa scholars (dge-shes) such as dGe-shes Dam-pa A-mes and Minyak sKyor-dpon bLo-bzang Yon-tan on the difficult problems that are part of the five subjects of monks who study dialectics, to the point where the scholars (dge-shes) could not say anything (in rebuttal). [54] The dGa'-ldan Khri Rin-po-che Dam-pa A-mes gave Rinpoche a work uniform that had been given by the traditional Tibetan government. He told Rinpoche: "You are a great scholar and like a garuda, the king of birds. If (you) stay at Lha-gdan,[128] you will preserve the wings of the scriptural authorization tradition. Minyak is like a clay pot and cannot protect your wings. Therefore, I ask it well of you if you would stay." The lead chanter[129] also asked this but Rinpoche replied:" The spiritual teachings in my land of Minyak have run down. The culture is not growing so the need of a teacher is greater than my staying. At any rate, I must return to my homeland." Rinpoche did not make a commitment to stay at Lha-gdan. The Minyak lead chanter kept asking for empowerments and scriptural authorization. Rinpoche asked to resign from being the tutor since more than a year had passed. He said it was important for all the older and younger monks with monasteries in dBu-tsang to return to their own monasteries.

All monks from Kham-gsum-grags monastery who had been in dBus-gtsang for some time such as lCang-ra bSod-nams don-grub, bLo-bzang dPal-ldan Tshe-dbang, 'Byor- dbus bSod-nams dPal-bzang, and A-ra Ye-shes rGya-mtsho returned home with Rinpoche. At the time they first headed out there were no more than four groups including the treasurer, lama's attendant, and religious services attendant, but this grew to more than ten. The Li-thang trader, A-'brug-tshang, traveled with them. After not too long a time, they arrived happily at Khams-gsum-grags Byams-chen Chos-'khor gLing. Monks and benefactors all came from everywhere to meet them. At the monastery there was a procession of monks and an elaborate reception. [55] The spiritual practitioners' and patrons' joy and confidence increased greatly and for the majority of those in the apartments around the courtyard, in the assembly hall, summer retreat house, treasury house and so forth. Speaking of the latter, the previous and later financial officers for Rinpoche included:

- The first treasurer Pha'u-thun A-'bum, imposing, tall and well-built, of good character, friendly to all, steady of mind, a man of few words.
- The treasurer Khu-bo Ye-shes, a monk at 'Ge-ba monastery was invited there. In physique he was very much like Rinpoche. His mind was pure in the monastery, but he took issue with extravagances. Except for guarding the cash, he took no joy in business affairs. Though he was pure in his vows, he liked weapons.
- bLo-bzang bZod-pa was appointed treasurer for some time. He was selfless, kind to his inferiors, got along with everyone, a person of straight character.
- LCang-ra bSod-nam Don-drub was tall and had a face like a mountain goat.[130] He knew little about business,

more of vulgar human conduct, was cowardly, so-so in his conduct.

- Lha-mgo Ka-rma rnNam-rgyal was younger, treasurer for a long period. Skilled in needlework, he sewed most of the seat cushions for the lama's residence (bla-brang) by himself. He sewed Rinpoche's clothing, the rug that went under [Rinpoche's horse] saddle and so forth. He was a person of few words, talented, a truthful person who got along with everyone.

- Mi-rag Rin-chen rGyal-mtshan was of medium height, had a beard, wore everyday monk's clothing, talked a lot, was shrewd, not too bad at guarding the finances, but tended to look after personal interests.

- A-mchod Ngag-dbang was very tall and of very pure mind at the monastery. He liked [56] small expenditures and took great care of the finances. He was a bit course in manners but a person of good character. Since he was a person who had come from another country (region), he did not really fall under the jurisdiction of the monastery.[131]

- bLo-bzang rGyal-mtshan[132] was short, plump, of very pure mind at the monastery. He was selfless[133] and spoke little. Timid, he did not have much skill in maintaining the finances but was a person of good character. All these previous treasurers have died. Since I was acquainted with them, I write this in commemoration for future generations.

Gangkar Rinpoche

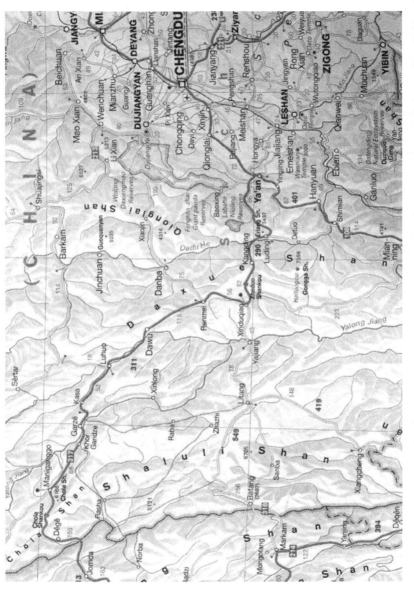

Map of part of Kham with Dege upper left corner, Kangding (Dartsendo) slightly to the right of center with Gongga Shan below.

Traveling two times to Greater China (Ma ha Tsi na) to spread the teachings of the sutras and tantras, to bring to spiritual maturity and liberate his students

Rinpoche was 43 in the Wood-Pig year of the 16th calendrical cycle (1935). Nor-lha Rin-po-che, a lama who performed ritual ceremonies or rites to remove difficulties[134] for the nation,[135] came to Dar-rtsi mdo in Khams. Gangkar Rinpoche was very delighted to meet him. bLa-ma Nor-lha who told him: "You really should come to China."

Nor-lha's general secretary, Han Da Cai, and other Chinese students asked him repeatedly: "You really ought to come to China."[136] Later, in any letters that Nor-lha wrote he would ask Rinpoche to come to China to teach, to be a spiritual doctor for people.

Nor-lha was born in 1876 in the Fire Mouse year of the 15th calendrical cycle in a home at a goat coral/encampment in a nice valley at the fort at Chab-mdo Ri-bo-che Rva-sha-chu.[137] He was 17 years older than Rinpoche. He was well-known as the Rva bLa-ma at the encampment due to his qualities. His mother was the daughter of his paternal aunt, in a family that had been lama attendants (rje drung) for seven generations. From the time he was very young he had earned the name "lama". He went to the school for religious study at the rNying-ma college at Ri-bo-che monastery, staying with the rJe-drung Byams-pa'i 'Byung-gnas bLa-ma. [58] From the time he was a child, he possessed supernormal powers and awareness. He completed his studies at Riboche monastery when he reached maturity and in the Earth-Pig year (1899) went with his teacher on spiritual pilgrimage to sPo-bo Padma-bkod.[138] Many signs of realization were shown. He found many pilgrimage sites for the first time (gnas sgo) and established a monastery on the A-'dra plain. The number of students and benefactors increased greatly. The sPo-bo ka: gnam sde-ba (chief) offered him all the monasteries of the high-pasturage plain. The monks rGya-mTsho and rDza-phud Kong-sprul were both appointed bosses by proxy. In the Fire-Sheep year (1907), he returned to his own monastery at Ri-bo-che. In the Iron-Dog year (1910) all the sPo-bo monasteries[139] were burned in fires started by monk soldiers[140] in that area. Nor-bla[141] Rinpoche was held prisoner of the local government (sDe-zhung) on account of his providing assistance to the Qing army. Getting free of the prison by various means, he went to China. In China, he had many students and became very well-known.[142] He met the leader of the nation at that time, Chiang Kai-shek (Jiang Jae Shi), who regarded him highly. Later Chiang came with the army to protect Dar-tsi-mdo. In the Wood-Pig year of the 16th calendrical cycle (1935) Nor-lha was given the position of Youth Leader (gtso-'dzin gzhon-pa) for the Tibetan government (bod-pa srid-gzhung) by the Red Army at dKar-mdzes. He received medical treatment at the Red Army Hospital but it was of no benefit and he died. His students Han Dva-tsha'i and others performed the funeral services. The heart, tongue, and eyes were left over (after the ceremonies) since they did not burn. The heart was known as the Venerable Tara who appeared by (her) self.[143]

The students of Nor-lha, eyes damp with tears, returned to China They requested help again and again. Since he was could not be indifferent to repeated requests for help, Rinpoche made a promise.

[59] In the Fire-Mouse year of the 16th calendrical cycle (1936) the treasurer bZod-pa, chief attendant (sol dpon) mKhyen-rab, astrologer (pra phab) bLa-ma Chos-grags, interpreter Man Kung Fa-shi, monks rGyal-mtshan and bSod-nams Tshe-ring went with Rinpoche as a party of seven to Dar-rtsi-mdo. Money to cover expenses for the journey was sent promptly by the head of the Chongqing bank, Director Pan, and Director Chen from Chongqing, so the party did not stay long at Dar-rtsi-mdo and went on to Chengdu. At Chengdu [Rinpoche] gave refuge,

empowerments and scriptural authorization for venerable *Tara, Avalokitesvara, Vajrayogini,* empowerments for bDe-mchog (*Cakrasamvara*) and rGyal-ba rgya-mtsho, authorization for consciousness transference, instruction on *phyag-chen* (*Mahamudra*) and the six doctrines of Naropa according to the Kam-tshang tradition. This was the first dissemination of deep teachings of the Kagyupa that would later spread throughout China. Students who requested teachings grew to more than 10,000. Among them were the great Army Commander Liu Shang, the great officer Pan Wun Ha and so forth. Many such requests for empowerments or authorization were made. After a few months, they went to Chongqing. Many students of Nor-lha who had been with Rinpoche before were there. He continued teaching deep rNying-ma ideas, the "Trilogy of texts on Easing the Mind" (Ngal-gso skor-gsum), "Pith Instructions of the Mother-Son" (sNying-thig ma-bu), the seven texts of Longchenpa, the direct approach (thod-brgal),[144] cutting through (khreg-chod),[145] the profound arcane rDzogs chen including special "Instructions from the Wisdom Teacher" (Ye-shes bla-ma). A festival that fell on the tenth day was held and together students and their teacher established the custom of making offerings at specific times and at large group gatherings. Benefactors such as Phan khru'u krang[146] frequently requested that rituals to remove difficulties be performed. There were marketplace empowerments for thousands of shopkeepers, vows of refuge, scriptural authorization for consciousness transference, [60] prayers necessary for keeping one's commitments and profound instructions on seed mantras for each deity. He gave deep teachings of the bKa'-brgyud- pa, the "*Mahamudra* – the Ocean of Ultimate Meaning" (Phyag-chen Nges-don rgya-mtsho), development phase of Vajrayogini according to the Kam-tsang bDe-mchog (*Cakrasamvara*) tradition, five protective circles teaching of Lhan-cig skyes-ma in the six doctrines of Naropa and the gCig-shes kun-grol (total liberation through unified awareness). In the Nyingmapa cycle of teaching there was instruction on the Khrid ye-shes bla-ma, "cutting through" (khregs-chod), "leaping high" (thod brgal), sNying-thig ma-bu, rDo-rje gro-lod, and the Ngal-gso skor-gsum.[147] Parts of the Kun-bzang bla-ma ("Teaching of My Perfect Teacher") were translated into Chinese. After several months at Chongqing, in the Fire-Ox year (1937), he got on a boat and reached Jiangxi Lushan by way of Nanchang and Changsha. He got off the boat at Jiangxi and, as he arrived in town, on the right and left sides of the road a huge crowd[148] of people had gathered to greet him. Hundreds of pretty young girls sang songs and tossed flowers. A band played various tunes as it lead soldiers in formation. Many monks lined up carefully to greet him with all kinds of offerings, pots of incense, pennants, parasols, bunches of auspicious symbols. Different kinds of leaders by the dozen[149] came in small cars, a great retinue greeting Rinpoche. The leaders of the Guomingtang, the young president of the republic, Li Zong Ren and the army commander Zhang Xue Liang[150] and others became his students. The main purpose in going to Jiang xi Lushan[151] was to set up an image of Nor-lha. Since this was the reason rolls of prayers were offered for the images being built at the Orgyan temple, they started to build a stupa (mchod-rten) before long. [61]

Rinpoche completed a proper survey and right away recruited many skilled Chinese builders. This "Awakening Stupa", with relics inside, was made of only steel and cement. It stood more than 15 meters high and was completed in just over six months. Relics were placed inside and many gold and silver offerings; hundreds of silver lamps inside the seat; tens of rolls of serge made in India; hundreds of rolls of high-quality silk; texts, *mantras* and *dharinis*; many sacred and holy relics placed in a vase. At completion, various jewels, all clothing regularly worn by Nor-lha, *mantras, dharinis* together with longer mantras were put in place in the core. *Dharinis* were also offered for the images of the O-rgyan temple and when they were finished, more extensive consecration rituals were conducted. Teachers and students all achieved what they had hoped for. While this was going on, ritual ceremonies were performed many times to turn around obstacles facing the country. In general, to keep in accord with the expectation of the students, he reckoned he would stay there for a few years. But after a year, the war of resistance against Japan had begun, and because of the unhappy times, he felt he had to return to Chongqing, traveling via Nanchang and Hunan Changsha.

At that time A-mdo Shes-rab rgya-mtsho was also living in China. Although the two learned persons had not actually met in person they kept in touch continuously. Shes-rab rgya-mtsho did not associate with many scholars but had a great interest in other views. He said:

[62]
"A mountain rises enveloped by an upper garment of <u>snow</u>.
A sage is busy with <u>pure</u> conduct.[152]
I have not seen him but delight in his words.
Even more, confident in what I know, I have a basis for understanding."

An ongoing series of letters ensued covering everything from compliments, praises, sutras, mantras to discussion of the political issues of the day.[153]

After more than a month of spiritual instructions at Chongqing, in 1939, in the Earth-Rabbit Year of the 16th calendrical cycle he happily returned to his own monastery via Chengdu. To all the monks, senior and junior, he gave religious garments and seven dollars; to each patron household great bundles of tea and ceremonial arrows with ribbons of five colors; to the surrounding monastic community without partiality, draperies that had been woven for the medicine deities and images of the Buddha. At the monastery, shrine objects of gold and silver, offerings of high-quality silk, musical instruments with precious stones, together with gold and silver images of the embodiment, speech, and awareness, one by one beyond reckoning or words, these offerings were presented by patrons and students from China. "This and this" they would say setting them forth like a shopkeeper keeping accounts, the many records noting what was required in the entry but not the important detail. Rinpoche had brought with him from Chengdu several thousand religious garments. To all the religious who had come from upper and lower parts of Minyak requesting spiritual teachings, novice or full vows for a monk, he gave each a garment as was the custom. He gave a new robe to each 2nd and 3rd-year student at the teaching college. Many Chinese university students and researchers from what is now Guangdong, Sichuan, and Beijing accompanied Rinpoche. I forget [all their] names now.[154] [63]

As the Sino-Japanese war was ending, Rinpoche had reached mid-life. In 1945, the Wood-Bird year of the 16th calendrical cycle, he was 53. During the winter, letters of invitation kept coming persistently from Huang He Qu, the head of the Finance Department of Yunnan Province, on behalf of Chinese students. The head of the Office of the Kham-Tibet Highway, a young man [named] Shao Fu Chen, due to his own good fortune, had invited [Rinpoche] and promised to provide traveling expenses and money for receptions for him so he could travel to China on two occasions. In the 9th Tibetan month of that year bLa-ma mKhyen-rab, who held the position of both treasurer and attendant, the translator Man kung Fa-shi, astrologer bLa-ma Chos-grags, the servant monks mGon-po,[155] bSod-nams, and Ngag-bang chos- grags, making up a total party of seven, left the monastery and went to Dar-rtse-mdo. There sPom-mda' sTobs-rgyas, Bya-rgod sTobs-ldan, dKar-mdzes Khang-gsar dPon-mo and other high ranking Tibetans came to meet Rinpoche and request many deep teachings, empowerments, and scriptural authorizations. sPom-mda' stobs-rgyas asked that a Chinese-Tibetan Bilingual Glossary be proofread. Back and forth questioning between Chinese workers and many reincarnated Tibetan lamas proceeded without interruption in this work.

After more than a month had past, Rinpoche, his attendant and the translator were carried in sedan chairs by servants on foot to Ya'an. When Rinpoche, his attendant, translator-servant arrived in Ya'an, they travelled onwards to Chengdu by car.

[64] After a few days some of the servants, taking items used in ritual offerings and cash, went by bus to Chengdu. At Chengdu, in a narrow street called Khr'ang yon, they stayed at sPo-tsi hPhu-shog sen[156] monastery. They were warmly greeted by the monastery master and Chinese Buddhist monks.[157] He was invited to Sichuan University and gave a talk on the five major and minor sciences. Zhang Yi Sun and many other professors paid him compliments. He went to the school for cultural relics and gave detailed explanations on the Tibetan relics, impressing all the students there. To General Pan Wen Hua, Army Commander Li and so forth, the master of the shop that made images and ritual instruments, Zhang Sun Fu, and many thousands of men and women in the market place he gave many deep teachings in the Nyingma cycle; on khreg-chod (cutting through) and thod-brgal (a leap aiming high); instruction in the phyag-chen (*Mahamudra*) cycle and on the six doctrines of Naropa. There were so many who requested the scriptural authorizations and teachings on consciousness transference ('pho ba), and thousands of students at each 'pho-lung[158] ceremony, it is difficult to recall exact numbers. At Krab ca'o su[159] and Wen shu yuan[160] many Chinese Buddhist monks requested teachings. After more than a month had past, he went by car to Chongqing where there was a joyous, happy, expansive welcome. He stayed at Khrang An Si monastery. The Buddha-image and temple at that monastery had been destroyed during the Sino-Japanese War. Although these had not been completely restored, many new living quarters had been built. Rinpoche, his attendant, and the translator stayed at one of the new houses. The [Tibetan] monks stayed with the Chinese Buddhist monks. [65] Because of guarantees[161] by both Tungsi Khran, the owner of the water delivery company, and the Chongqing Bank, many

63

ceremonies to remove the obstacles facing the country (rim gro) were conducted there. Whatever was appropriate (for his audience), he gave deep teachings, instructions and empowerments to many leaders such as Li Zong Ren, the young President and leader of the Guomingtang, Chongqing Mayor Zhang Zhu ren, Director Qiu Hua, He Qu,[162] and their wives.[163] The Chinese lama Tshug Sa Hoshang, Rung zhing Hoshang,[164] Man kung Hoshang, Yo min Hoshang and scholarly novice monks started the transcription and free translation of many Kagyupa and Nyingmapa Buddhist teachings. He gave venerable *Tara* and *Avalokitesvara* empowerments, refuge vows and scriptural authorization for consciousness transference to nearly 100,000 people in the marketplaces.

The head of the Chongqing Ceramics Factory had been a student of Rinpoche in the past. Although he had died, his sons, used to going before a Buddha-image, became his students. A statue of Rinpoche had been built previously and even more were made. He gave many Nyingma teachings to Wang Jia Qi,[165] professor at the Chongqing Nor-bla Study Group (nor bla'i slob tshog). When (the professor) was given a golden-colored cotton Pandita hat indicating the three collections of scriptures,[166] it was announced that the professor was following in Nor-lha's footsteps. Students and teacher on the tenth day of the lunar month held an elaborate teaching gathering. They went to visit a wool fabric factory, cotton fabric factory, and pasturage areas. After a few months, Huang He Qu went ahead to Yunnan to make arrangements. The lama, together with his retinue and General Zhang, flew from the airport on the Qongqing River to Kunming in Yunnan. At the Kunming airport Huang He Qu [66] was there with a bunch of students to enthusiastically greet [Rinpoche]. The whole group stayed at Huang He Qu's house. He gave empowerments, scriptural authorization, and instructions many times to several wives of generals and officials of the province. The seed mantras of the protective deities, texts for many recitation practices and parts of the

"Very Clear Spiritual Practices of the bKa' brgyud" were translated into Chinese. Over many days he gave empowerments and scriptural authorization to Tsu'u Ca'an Kphu, the head of many cotton fabric factories and to the chief of the gold market. Ceremonies to remove obstacles (rim gro) were held. At Yunnan University he gave a talk on the five major and minor sciences, and was given a meal.[167] While he was staying there, the Mongolian lama rDo-rje Seng-ge and his students stayed with Rinpoche. The lama made several requests for scriptural authorization and commentary on deep teachings of the Kagyupa such as the "Six Doctrines of Naropa", and especially Nyingmapa teachings on 'cutting through' (khregs-chod), 'leaping high' (thod-brgal), the collection of instructions on the Ye-shes bla-ma and the "Deep Teaching on the Automatic Liberation by the Contemplation of the Peaceful and Wrathful Deities'. As a steadfast trusting confidence had arisen in him, rDo-rje Seng-ge gave Rinpoche the instruments he and his students used in religious offerings...

He was invited to a most beautiful monastery, Kab mi'o si.[168] A rain of teachings from the ordinary method fell on the Chinese Buddhist monks. The monastery gave him a large meal as was the custom of Chinese Buddhist monks. While visiting Kunming Lake, they went to the Lung yu'u[169] hot springs bathing facility. He gave the empowerment and scriptural authorization for consciousness transference many times to thousands of people in the marketplaces. After a stay of more than three months, he went by plane to Chongqing. There was a grand reception for him at the airport. He stayed at the places he had been before. [67]

In not too much time, because of repeated entreaties from student leaders, the central government of the Guomingtang held a meeting to honor the spiritual teachers (bla ma) of the country. Chen Lung Fu[170] was the chief organizer of the event. [Student] leaders who attended the meeting were Director Yun, Director Qiu, Board Director Pan, Huang He Qu and so forth, the secretary for the delegates of Chiang Kai-shek, delegates of some universities and many who may have been students. There was a very elaborate reception. He was given an ornament with four golden lions on the corners and the title "Friend who Increases the [Buddhist] Teachings, All-knowing Master of Meditation (bsam-gtan)."[171] The leaders and students praised Rinpoche's knowledge and so on. He gave a speech to express his gratitude to the central government and this speech is highly regarded in Tibetan Buddhist teachings and considered an important talk. They made up four rows of seats and following the foreign custom of providing food and entertainment for guests, many young women sang songs and played different sorts of music for more than half a day before they finished. In the summer, Chongqing gets very hot. So he went to a monastery at Lifu Shan to escape the heat, about 40 miles to the southwest of Chongqing. From time to time he would go by sedan chair to town to give empowerments or spiritual teachings. The teachings would begin right away whenever he got to Chongqing. He worked without break at the promotion of Buddhism for the benefit of all sentient beings.

[68] He consolidated his retinue. Four monks including the astrologer Chos-grags returned, each to his own monastery.[172] In the first month of the Fire-Pig Year of the 16th calendrical cycle (1947), [Rinpoche's] party of four, including his attendant, translator, and student Fu Yaolung, left Chongqing. They traveled to all the major cities of China including Hangzhou, Nanjing, Beijing, and Shanghai. He continued teaching the profound doctrines of non-sectarian Tibetan philosophical systems. Most of the reincarnated lamas of Tibet living in China paid their respects and requested teachings. Specifically, he gave all the profound teachings of the oral and textual traditions of the bKa-(brgyud-pa) and rNying (ma-pa) to those students who were ready for them. These included the bKa' brgyud teachings Ocean of Ultimate Meaning (Nges-don rgya-mtsho), Lamp of Ultimate Meaning (Nges-don sgron-me), Simultaneously emerging developmental process (bsKyed-rim lhan-cig skyes-ma), Developmental Process of the Non-Duality of

Awareness and Vital Energy (rDzogs-rim rlung-sems gnyis-med), sGampopa's Jewel Ornament of Liberation, biography of Milarepa, and the methods for offerings and prayers to the ocean of Dharma guardians. The Nyingma teachings included the series on the Profound Pure Manifestation (zab-mo dag-snang), Sky Teaching (gnam-chos), teachings in the Heart Essence Mind Treasure (sNying-thig dgongs-gter) series, rDzogs-chen cycle, mind section of the tradition from Bairotsana, the Vast expanse section (kLong-sde), and the Instruction Section (man-ngag-sde) from Vimalamitra. As well as the cycle of teachings on old and new revealed texts, he started the translation of the writings of kLong-chen-pa into Chinese. In the country of Mahacina (greater China) he established a solid basis for teaching arcane doctrines. He explained the method behind key instructions to Chinese novice-monk scholars and delegates of masters of monasteries, integrating this with the essential inner meaning in the Sutra of the Definite Explanation of the Intent (mDo-dgongs nges-'grel), Asanga's Five Treatises on Levels (Sa-sde lnga), Maitreya's Five Texts (Byams-pa'i chos-sde-lnga), and biography of the Thang-seng bla-ma.[173] Everyone showed their great respect. Most stayed with the lama. [69]

He made the teachings of *sutras* and *tantras* according to the Tibetan traditions shine like the sun in China. In the autumn of the Earth-Ox year of the 16th calendrical cycle (1949) when he ws 57, at Ya'an, while on the road to Dar-rtsi-mdo from Chengdu, Rinpoche's chief attendant, mKhyen-rab, who had not been away from Rinpoche for more than 30 years, died. Rinpoche was deeply saddened by this. He conducted the transference of consciousness ceremony and made extensive prayers. At the time of the cremation (zhugs 'bul) auspicious signs and marks beyond imagining appeared on the body. Rinpoche said: "It is difficult these days to find someone so loyal. In just one day he is no longer with us." Saying this, his eyes filled with tears. For a long time he sat without moving. At that time, the boss from his own monastery, treasurer, monastic officials, leading patrons, chiefs of the area, together with other leaders and many

67

horsemen had gone to greet Rinpoche at Ya'an. A lot of pack animals were brought to transport his possessions. Rinpoche traveled by sedan chair with those who had come to greet him. Along the way at the towns of Tianquan (Then-chen) and Shiyang (Hri-yang,)[174] Chinese students and their leaders lined up to greet him. At Luding (lCags-zam-kha) there were more than 1000 people who came down from Dar-rtsi-mdo to greet him, together forming a long column. When they reached Dar-rtsi-mdo, close to and to the east of the town, because it is the door to China, the monks of the Dar-rtsi-mdo monasteries[175] at the Waseng valley, from rDo-rje drag, Sa-skya, lNga-mchod,[176] Lha-mo rtse,[177] Ngor, rDor-drag,[178] greeted him in an elaborate procession with blowing conches and oboe-like instruments (rgya-gling).

[70] The leaders of Dar-mdo, shopkeepers and nobles (sku drag) alike, welcomed [Rinpoche] with white silk *kata* (offering scarves). Many people in the marketplace paid their respects and sought a hands-on type of blessing from the lama. Thousands of people were there. He got away from the crowd gradually to stay at Kha-ba rGya-mtsho tshang-sar. He gave lots of gifts to the aristocrats and tea provision leaders ('byed mang ja) at the monasteries; spiritual teachings to many who were already making progress in their practice; and detailed instructions and empowerments to his students. In about 20 days he went to his own monastery, Khams-gsum-grags. After a few days, people of the area, monks and reincarnated lamas from the monastery welcomed [him] with boundless joy. He was happy to return to Khams-grags. At his monastery and its branches he gave alms, rice gruel, and tea to the monks who had gathered there for over seven days. He gave to each monk red and gold colored religious garments and silver money (yuan or ta-sgor), to benefactors large bricks of tea and bows with five-colored pieces of silk attached, to non-sectarian Minyak monasteries high-quality silk, and appropriate presents such as tea that would be offered as an alm (mang ja). Chinese students who came with Rinpoche at that time included

Hong He Qu, Wu Tsi Qi, Hu Ye Tao[179] with their wives and children,[180] Cu Sa Fa-shi of Ya'an, the talented Ma khung Fa-shi, together with Yon-min Fa-shi. They stayed with Rinpoche, received teaching (chos zhu) and made efforts at practicing meditation. In some, signs of realization (chos 'grub) came forth. Wu'u Tsi chi died at the old Gangkar monastery.

After liberation, accepting leadership in the Party and continuously expanding Tibetan culture

[71] Throughout his life Rinpoche was very busy with the three pure activities of teaching, debating, writing and the three very pure deeds of empowerment, scriptural authorization and instruction. Because he became the teacher for all Minyak doctors, he was always providing medical treatment for many lay people and monks. It is said that one corrupts [a physician's] commitments if one purifies by medicine but avoids what is not clean, so he checked a patient's pulse and urine himself. He gave whatever medicine was necessary to all sick people without regard for their ability to pay. For these reasons many came to him for treatment. Each calendar year he did calculations for Phan-bde bKra-shis, bLa-ma Padma chos-'phel, and Mi-rag phrin-las because he had taken on this responsibility. He never made a mistake whether there would or would not be an eclipse of the sun or moon, whether the eclipse would be total or partial. For that reason, he was the "king of Minyak astrologers."

When Rinpoche reached the age of 58 in the Iron-Tiger year of the 16th calendrical cycle (1950), in the Tibetan 3rd month, the Khams[181] region was peacefully liberated. [72] In the six month of that year Rinpoche said: "Now, liberation for the entire country is almost complete. Even as each region is liberated, a new government with new leaders has been appointed. It would not be right if I did not go to meet them." Together with a small entourage he went to Dar-rtsi-mdo. He exchanged silk scarves with the leaders of the party, government, and army: Political Commisar Miao Fu Zhu, Chairman Sangs-rgyas Ye-shes,[182] and Commander Fan Zhi Zhong. He stayed on in Dar-rtsi-mdo giving some empowerments and ritual permissions to students. Because he was well-known throughout all regions, nationally and internationally, many leaders of the Guomingtang were his students and there were some Chinese students at his monastery. Because of these various reasons and conditions, he was forced to stay in a "comfortable" prison ('jam btson).[183] He underwent intense questioning that continued for more than 10 months. It looked like there would be no end to the pressure on him. But gold is just gold. Even while everything was being looked into and carefully examined, his complexion became more and more clear.[184] Why was this? Not too much later, like the moon becoming free of clouds, he happily returned to his monastery. All the teachers (lama), students, patrons met him anew like mother and child separated for a long time, relaxed in sheer pleasure of great happiness and joy. Students at the teaching college strived in their studies, (now) happy and free of anxiety. All spiritual activities of the monastery came back to what they had been before. Even for the lama the deep teachings at times were like an unending rain of nectar, like the steady rain of the rainy season. In the Water-Sheep year (1952) more than 80 Chinese students who had been designated "leads" by Yu Dao Quan, the great professor at The Central Nationalities' University (Krung dbyang Mi rigs slob grva chen mo), came to Khams-gsum-grags Byams-chos-'khor gling to study with[185] Rinpoche. [73] They studied general Tibetan culture, specifically Rinpoche own writings, the 'Phags-stod commentary, Aphorisms of the Sa-skya Pandita,[186] instructions on Tibetan grammatical science.[187] They had instruction from student teachers such as the sDe-dge dPal spungs Tshe-sgrub,[188] Tshul-khrims zla-ba, and Nam-mkha'i Nor-bu, the bLo-gter sPrul-sku who was given a recommendation by Bya-rgod sTobs-ldan. After about a year had passed, the students, all goals fulfilled, paid their respects to Rinpoche and went back to Beijing.

In the Water-Snake Year (1953) The Central Nationalities' University sent a letter to the Dar-mdo Autonomous Region government inviting Rinpoche to Beijing. At the command of the youthful president of the Dar-mdo Autonomous Region, Li Chun Fang, Minyak Gonpo, an education cadre, was put in charge of the teacher's invitation. Although this came during an inauspicious year (skeg thog), the lama enthusiastically accepted the invitation. Together the student, teacher, and Ngag-dbang Nor-bu,[189] a servant who had held the position of chief attendant for six Tibetan months, went to Dar-rtsi-mdo. Not much later, they went to the Central Nationalities' University in Beijing. He stayed there for nearly 3 years, teaching Tibetology. He was asked to translate documents (yig cha) from the first National People's Congress into Tibetan. He answered questions sent from around the world concerning Tibetology and gave empowerments and spiritual teachings to students in Beijing. [74] After completing each cycle of activities including discussion about Buddhist teachings with other scholars such as mKhas-dbang Tshe-tan zhabs-drung,[190] gSung-rab rgya-mtsho, and the Chinese Tibetan scholar Fan Ze Fa-shi, at the end of the Wood-Sheep year (1955) he went back to Dar-rtsi-mdo. He stayed at the dKar-mdzes Tibetan People's Autonomous Prefecture Political Discussion House. To some officials and reincarnated lamas who were diligent in their work he taught Tibetan grammar, the <u>Sum-rtags</u>. To those who had great confidence, Bya-rgod stobs-ldan and so forth, he gave deep teachings on the cycle of teachings on bringing arcane teachings into lived experience. He participated many times in discussions about student Tibetan text books. When he wasn't doing this would go back to his own monastery and give deep teachings without interruption to his students and benefactors.

When the rGyal-dbang (Karmapa) Rang-byung Rig-pa'i rDo-rje was returning from Beijing, they met up at Dar-rtsi-mdo.[191] As his tutor, Gangkar Rinpoche had the duty to give him essential advice whenever they met. Rinpoche went together with all the monks, young and old, from his monastery to Minyak Ra-rNga-kha (Xinduqiao). There he met the Karmapa.[192] They spent three days very happily together. The Karmapa said repeatedly that it was important that [Rinpoche] accompany him to India from dBu- tsang, with an excuse of it being good for his health. Rinpoche did not make any promises. As it came close to the time the Karmapa would leave, the bond in the student teacher relationship got stronger and stronger so it seemed like they would not be able to part from one another. The lama watched and waved his hand as the Karmapa's car disappeared from view. [75] The Karmapa waved back from his car window, saying: "Come with me. Come with me.", and looking back again and again, left.

Karmapa Rang-byung Rig-pa'i rDo-rje and
Gangkar Rinpoche

Rinpoche arranged the enthronement of the incarnation of the dPal-spungs 'Jam-dbyangs mkhyen-brtse, establishing a connection as his first tutor.[193] He mediated a bitter dispute [between nomads] at sDe-dge. He worked on a commentary on the <u>Sum-rtags</u> and other [projects] as a literary Tibetan cadre at the Text Translation House and the Dkar-mdzes News House, never stopping in the continuing work of spreading Tibetan culture. [76]

His passing into freedom from suffering and the situation of his writings and his students

When Rinpoche was 64 on the 14th day of the 12th month of the Fire-Snake Year of the 16th calendrical cycle (Feb.; 1957), at the Dar-rtsi-mdo Prefecture Political Discussion[194] House, after receiving permission for a one month leave of absence , he bid farewell with white silk scarves to dBu-khrid Ngag-dbang rgya-mtsho and others. He had a final meeting with all his comrades at the Political House. He left the bed and sitting chair he used at the Political House as they were, placing a white scarf on each. He said this was for the connection with his attendant Ngag [dbang] nor [bu]. The significance of the gesture was a metaphor for his not coming back there again. Then, while on the way back to his own region, he gave a final audience and hand blessing (phyag dbang) to many male and female devotees. As he rode his horse up the rGya-gzar valley, the stones seemed to come up to meet him, and follow him as he passed. At the top of each pass, he got down from riding and made prayers for good fortune. He told all the junior and senior monks who met him on his return to his monastery: "It is important to have an elaborate assembly unlike anything before. There is a special connection very important for the "nine-fold great offering" (dgu gtor-chen-mo) this year. Clearly understand that the gathering for this "nine-fold great offering" is for the last time."

[77] Then, following Rinpoche's wishes, they got together all that was used in making offerings, silk and precious [objects] and displayed all offerings made of gold and silver. At the gathering there were many alms and offerings of tea. When the most excellent nine offering cakes (gtor-ma) were being brought to the assembly, at that moment the portion of all our merit gained from discipline was complete. In the deep gloom of the five degenerations, darkness spreading everywhere, the sun of the Buddha's teachings, was close to hiding secretly in the western mountains. In the evening at 11 o'clock on the 28th day of 12 month (March, 1957) in the Fire-Snake year of the 16th calendrical cycle, he gave instructions to ease the minds of younger students, at each student house. With great gladness of spirit (thugs-dgyes) he linked vital energy (rlung sbyor), settling the energy flows with the seven-point posture of Vairocana, his mind (dgongs pa) merging into the vast expanse of meaning.[195]

Then the banner of the bKa' brgyud pa teachings fell. The young male students' root parent passed away. The sun set for the confident. The scholars lost a friend who would talk with them. The sorrow and suffering of people at times like this cannot be expressed in words.

Up to now it has been 40 years since the death of [my] root teacher. Since (this time) has passed, for me and other students sadness has gone and is no more. The smiling face of [my] teacher and how he acted arises clearly in my mind. When I was 34 I was left a child, separate from his teacher. Now I am 74.

[78] There is no getting around relying on old records as a guide. Rinpoche's corpse did not move from the state of focus at the time of death and was placed in a container. Various kinds of precious sand (bye ma), (a mixture of) mostly saffron (gur gum), sweet-smelling herbs, sea and other kinds of salt were applied. Mkhan-po Phan-bde bkra-shis took care of the body, made dedication prayers and put on a head ornament and various clothing symbolizing the connection of being with and for others. At Chengdu a *stupa* (mchod-rten) of superior quality and about two stories high was built, ornamented with copper, silver, and gold. The dKar-mdzes Tibetan Language News (bod yig gsar 'gyur) proclaimed that (with) the "death of the Gangkar incarnation, placing [the body] in a *stupa* is in accordance with Tibetan Buddhist tradition." During the completion of building the *stupa*, the house for the corpse was finished according to standards. As the corpse was being carried to the *stupa*, when it was thought to be the right time to place the corpse in the *stupa*, four protest[196] campaigns had begun. All property of the monastery was seized by the government. All the sacred texts (gsung rab) were burned, monks forced to give up their robes. Under those circumstances, the corpse had to be taken to a cemetery. In the class struggle, good monks, devoted patrons went into hiding, what had been stable was smashed. On orders from above inquiries were carried out many times. Devoted individuals, at the risk of their lives, hid sacred relics in caves, beneath trees or in the ground. Having wrapped in silk the human bones from the cemetery and leaving substitutes in their place, through various means people were able to conceal them. Now these are the most important relics of the monastery. If this image is seen by one who is filled with confidence, a light shines in the heart. It is clear that there is much good in seeing it.

[79] Nowadays, there is a steady flow of people from all over who come to pay respect to the remains (relics).

In the series of religious texts that [Rinpoche] wrote are, specifically, the:

'Phags-bstod-kyi 'grel-pa
dBu-ma'i mtha-dpyod lta-ba'i yig-'byed
rGyal-rong dGe-bshes Karma Nges-don-gyi dri-lan mKhas-
    pa'i mgul-rgyan
sPyod-'jug 'grel-pa mjug-ma rdzogs-pa
Phar-phyin chos-'khor rnam-bzhag
bKa' bstan-bcos-kyi rnam-bzhag
Byams-pa sangs-rgyas yin-min-gyi rnam-bzhag
dNgos-brgyad don-bdun-cu'i spyi-don sum-rtags bsdu-don
    shes-rab sgron-me
rGyan-rug mchog-gnyis-kyi bstod-pa in the cycle of "praise
    works".[197]

There were many "cleansing" writings such as the Gangs-dkar bsang-yig and rGyab- ri rdo- rje la-rtse'i bsang-yig (Purification on the peak for rGyab-ri rdo-rje);[198] the cycle of teachings on (sacred) places such as the Gangs-dkar gnas-bshad dad-pa'i sa-bon;[199] writing in the cycle of rules such as the rDo-rje mdud-pa, the rules of Khams-gsum grags byams-chen chos-'khor gling, dedication prayers, regular prayers, offering prayers, ritual offerings for propitiation purposes (gser skyems), free discussions on various subjects (tshogs-bshad 'bel-gtam), official letters (chab-shog)[200], letters and so forth : all together they would take up 4 or five volumes (po ti). Apart from a few texts carved on wood blocks at his monastery or at sDe-dge dpal-spungs, and the Sum-btags bsdus-don shes-rab sgron-me which was printed by the Sichuan People's Publishing House, nowadays there is little to look for, little time needed to compile what is left. Not only have the books been lost because they were burned, but even Rinpoche's medical kit, precious unprocessed medical materials, rhinoceros horn, elephant tusk (ivory) and so forth was thrown down the toilet. [80] As Sapan has said:
"Proficiency is elegant in the wise, but how is a fool to understand it?

Sandalwood is made precious with gold; look how a fool turns it into charcoal!"

It seems that the prophecies are like these words. As is said:[201]

"Stairs to climb to the good house of the wise,[202]
Oceans that gather the rivers of experience,
Clear mirrors for a world passed away,
Alas, are destined for a realm with no point of reference."

For the holy people, reincarnated teachers of the Sa(skya), dGe(lugs), bKa(brgyud), rNying(ma) who studied in his presence and Chinese officials, great teachers Mo Fa-shi and so forth, even if mentioned before, if one were to compile a list of them all together, first there is:

Lord of the bKa'-brgyud pa, rGyal-dbang Karmapa Rang-byung rig-pa'i rdo-rje, gNas- nang dPa'-bo Rin-po-che, rGyal-tshab Rin-po-che, Phag-mo-Ri[203] sPrul-sku, dPal-spung 'Jam-dbyangs mKhyen-brtse, 'Jang sGrol-dkar sPrul-sku, sPrul-sku Tshe-dpag and so on.

In the gSang-sngags Nyingmapa: Lord Ba: gNas-mchog-sprul Rig-'dzin dPa'-bo Nyi-ma 'od-'bar, Brag-mkhar sPrul-sku Kun-bzang, Brag-mkhar sPrul-sku Pad-rdor, sPrul-sku brTson-'grus mThar-phyin and so on.

Lamas and sprul-sku of the Sa-skya-pa including: sPrul-sku bsTan-pa'i Nyi -ma of the Gha thar-lam monastery, Ri-khud sPrul-sku, sPrul-sku Kun-bzang and so forth.

Lamas and sprul-sku of Ri-bo dga'ldan[204] including Chos-kyi rGya-mtsho, the most excellent incarnation of sKyid-gling monastery
[81]
sPrul-sku 'Jam-dbyangs skal-ldan, Minyak sKyor-dpon bLo-bzang Yon-tan,[205] Lha-rams dGe-bshes dKon-mchog bsTan-

'dzin,[206] mTshan-zhabs-pa dGe-bshes Ngag-dbang Phan-bde, dGe-bshes rGyal-mtshan, dGe-bshes Ngag-dbang Byams-pa and so on.

Among the Tibetan officials and aristocracy were Bragg'yab sPom-mda' sTobs-rgyas, Khyung-rab mDa'-dpon, rGya-rgod sTobs-ldan, rGyal-rong Khro-skyabs rGyal-po rDo-rje dPal-bzang, dKar-mdzes Khang-gsar dPon-mo bDe-chen dBang-mo, Dar-mdo lCags-la rGyal-po Phun-tshogs, Minyak Kha-dbus dPon'Jam-dbyangs, O-rong-shis bZang-'phel dPon dBang-phyug and Thub-bstan, Minyak stod 'Brog-pa'i dPon[207] Hor-dpal-dkon, Dar-mdor Phvya-dpon Sung bLa- ma and so forth. I am listing only some of the leaders since I cannot list them all. For the most part I have mentioned above the senior Chinese students. Sun Shu Wen, a woman who took layperson's vows, is from Beijing and lives in Taiwan. She established a Kar (brgyud) monastery in Taiwan,[208] established a teaching community, spread the Kar) brgyud teachings and [gained] many students. At the time of repairing the dGangs monastery, she gave much friendship and help. Now it has stood for 100 years.

"Manufacturing, healing, epistemology, inner meaning, grammatical science, poetry, rhetoric, composition, drama, astrology - five sciences reach the peak where they are joined - and through the power of the wise, spread out on the earth."

[82] Final Thoughts

Now I have have reached the limits of what I remember of the life of my teacher and finish writing. The pure perception (dag snang gi ngor) and direct realization (nyams snang) of the best of Rinpoche's students, times when Rinpoche sLob-dpon Pad-ma, Thugs-rje chen-po, rJe-btsun sgrol-ma, rDo-rje 'chang and so forth could be seen as real, and the prophecy in the prophetic text of the revealer of treasures 'Gro-'dul gling- pa that there would be an incarnation from the 25 disciples of Guru Rinpoche of Shud-bu dPal-gyi Seng-ge: although these were not ordinary, are what's left for now.[209]

When I was a child, when the empowerment for Thugs-rje chen-po was being given in the assembly hall to the monks and lamas, though a few of the reincarnated lamas saw as real the 11-headed Lord, I saw a little (image of Thugs-rje chen-po) above the head of the lama get farther and farther away until it faded away and I couldn't see it any more. Rinpoche recognized sacred places for the first time, left footprints in stone, and stones were seen following the steps of his horse as I have mention above. I am uncomfortable with heaps of praise concerning events in the life of my teacher. For that reason, therefore, don't criticize the writing if I am different from others [in that regard]. There were those making compliments when our teacher Sakyamuni was alive, and in taking measure of him as a man called him the "best among men", the "chief of bipeds", and so forth. I am innocent [of such talk] in this context.

[83] When I think of the kind words of my teacher, does it not help to return a little kindness? By cherishing the unbroken continuity of the lama's work, it is important to strive at the work of spreading Tibetan culture. In that regard, this is what I do. Through repeated urgings, again and again, of many *vajra* brothers and friends from ceremonies (mchod grogs), this book has emerged from a sincere desire I had earlier to write a general life story of my teacher. I have become a worldly servant with many work responsibilities. Apart from my experiences, there is little data to work with. With a relaxed mind, when I remember the kind face of my teacher, I remember nothing else and am about to faint. Through various causes and conditions, up to now, the writing has been delayed. Now I am tired from the telling. My eyes are bleary, hands shaky. My memory is breaking down. Even if my mind should suddenly go, there is still something written down now. Since a few wrong words or contradictions in meaning are impossible to avoid, for those with understanding and open eyes, I ask from my heart that you not just find fault, but intend to make corrections.

May the good that has come from the efforts here
Become the cause for well-being throughout the land, happiness for beings,
Pure ethics, discipline and harmony in the spiritual community,
And medicine for the teachings and sentient beings.

Written in the Fire-Mouse year of the 17th calendrical cycle (1996) at the capital, Beijing,[210] by Gangkar Rinpoche's lowly student, Minyak Gonpo, 74, 40 years after the death of his teacher.

༄༅། །གངས་དཀར་གྱི་གནས་ཡིག་དང་གནས་འདྲེན་སྐྱབས་ཀྱི་ཕན་ཡོན་
མདོར་བསྡུས་དང་པའི་ས་བོན་ཞེས་བྱ་བ་བཞུགས་སོ། །

གངས་དཀར་རིན་པོ་ཆེས་བརྩམས།

The seed of devotion: a pilgrim's guide to Gangkar with a synopsis of benefits found at sacred sites

By Gangkar Rinpoche

འདིར་བོད་ཀྱི་གནས་ཆེན་བཞིའི་ཡ་གྱལ་གནས་མཆོག་འབོ་གངས་དཀར་འདི་ཉིད་ཀྱི་
གནས་ཀྱི་ཡོན་ཏན་དང་གནས་འདུས་ཀྱི་ཕན་ཡོན་མདོར་བསྡུས་ཚམ་ཞིག་སྟོན་གྱི་ཡིག་
རྙིང་རྣམས་ལས་བཏུས་ནས་ཚིག་སྟོར་མཛེས་ཁྲིགས་སྤངས་ཏེ་གོ་སླ་བའི་ངག་གིས་
འཆད་པ་ལ་གཉིས། གནས་ཀྱི་ཡོན་ཏན་སྤྱིར་བཤད་པ་དང་། གནས་འདུས་སྐབས་
ཕན་ཡོན་བྱེ་བྲག་ཏུ་བཤད་པའོ། །

དང་པོ་ནི། སངས་རྒྱས་གཉིས་པ་པདྨ་འབྱུང་གནས་ཀྱི་ལུང་བྱང་དུ་མ་ནས་གནས་
འདིའི་མཚན་ཉིད་ཞིབ་ཏུ་གསུངས་ཤིང་ཆེ་བའི་ཡོན་ཏན་ལ་བསྔགས་པར་མཛད་པ་དང་
། ཐམས་ཅད་མཁྱེན་པ་ཀརྨ་པ་རོལ་པའི་རྡོ་རྗེ་གོང་མའི་ཕོ་བྲང་དུ་བྱུང་ལམ་ནས་མར་
ཡེབས་པའི་ཚེ། སྤྲོ་ལ་གི་ན་འབོ་གངས་དཀར་ཡོད་དེ་སྒྲུབ་གནས་ཁྱད་པར་དུ་འཕགས་
པ་ཡིན་

The seed of devotion: a pilgrim's guide to Minyak Gangkar with a synopsis of benefits found at sacred sites

'Bo Gangs dkar is an exceptional part of the four great ranges of Tibet. This is a compilation, a brief explanation from the old texts of the past on the capabilities of this place and the benefits that are inherent here. Having given up on an elegant writing style, there are two we can easily talk about: a general explanation on the qualities of this place and a more specific explanation on the benefits gathered here.

First, from many pure traditions of the deep treasures of the 2nd Awakened One (Buddha) Padmakara, there are very detailed texts on the main features of this place and high praises for its great capabilities. When the one with total knowledge, Karmapa Rol-pa'i rDo-rje, was coming down from the northern route to his upper residence, he said: "In the south is 'Bo Gangs-dkar. It is the best place, in particular, for spiritual practice.

པས་རང་རེ་ཡར་འོང་དུས་དེར་སྐོམ་དུ་འགྲོ་གསུངས་ནས་བསྐུལ་བས་བརྟོད་མཛད་ཅིང་།

ཡར་ལམ་གནས་འདིར་ཞབས་ཀྱིས་བཅགས་ཤིང་བྱིན་གྱིས་བརླབས་པ་དང་། གཞན་

ཡང་རྣལ་འབྱོར་གྱི་དབང་ཕྱུག་ཞིག་པོ་གཉིས་མེད་རྡོ་རྗེ། གྲུབ་པའི་དབང་པོ་ཀུན་

དགའ་རྒྱལ་མཚན། གྲུབ་ཆེན་ཐང་སྟོང་རྒྱལ་པོ། མཁས་གྲུབ་ཆེན་པོ་འཛམ་དབྱངས་

གྲགས་པ་སོགས་སྐྱེས་ཆེན་དུ་མས་ཞབས་ཀྱིས་བཅགས་ཤིང་རྫུ་འཕྲུལ་གྱི་བཀོད་པ་

དང་གྲུབ་པའི་རྟགས་རྡོ་མཚར་བ་དུ་མས་གནས་བྱིན་གྱིས་བརླབས་པར་མཛད་པའི་

སྐྱོངས་འདིའི་རི་དབུ་འདི་ནི། ཕྱི་ལྟར་ན་ཐ་མལ་མིའི་སྣང་ངོར་རི་དབང་ལྷུན་པོ་ལ་

འགྲན་བཟོད་པའི་གངས་དཀར་ཤེལ་གྱི་ཅོད་པན་ཆེས་མཐོ་བས་རི་ཕྲན་ཐམས་ཅད་

ཟིལ་གྱིས་གནོན་ཞིང་། ཕྱིའི་དབྱིབས་རྒྱལ་སྲིད་སྣ་བདུན་དང་བཀྲ་ཤིས་རྟགས་བརྒྱད་

ཀྱི་རྣམ་པར་བཀྲ་བའི་དགེ་མཚན་གྱིས་མཛེས་ཤིང་། འཛམ་གྱིང་གི་ཤིང་སྣ་ཐམས་ཅད་

ཚང་བ་དང་། གདུགས་དང་བ་དན་སོགས་མཆོད་རྫས་ཀྱི་རྣམ་པ་རྒྱན་མི་ཆད་པ་དང་།

རི་དེའི་མགུལ་ན་རང་བྱུང་འོད་ཀྱི་དར་པོ་ཆེ་ཁ་དོག་ཅེར་ཡང་སྣང་བ་དུས་གསུམ་གྱི་

སངས་རྒྱས་རྣམས་ཀྱིས་རབ་ཏུ་གནས་ཤིང་བྱིན་གྱིས་བརླབས་པ་དང་སྲོབ་པར་འགྱུར་

པ་འདི་ཉིད་འཕྲལ་དུ་མཐོང་ན་ལས་སྒྲིབ་སྒྲུབ་པའི་རྟགས་དང་། བསྐལ་མ་ཐག་ཏུ་

མཐོང་མ་ནུས་ན་ལས་ལོན་གྱི་སྒྲིབ་པ་ཤས་ཆེ་བའི་རྟགས་ཡིན་ལས་ཕྱག་བསྐོར་ཡིག་

བརྒྱ་སོགས་ལ་འབད་དགོས་པ་དང་། དེ་ཡང་དཀར་པོ་མཐོང་ན་ཞི་བའི་ལས་འགྲུབ་ཆེ

རིང་ནད་མེད་ཕྱི་མ་བདེ་བ་ཅན་དུ་སྐྱེ་བ་དང་། སེར་པོ་མཐོང་ན་བསོད་ནམས་ལོངས་

སྤྱོད་ཆེ་ཞིང་རྒྱས་པའི་ལས་འགྲུབ། དམར་པོ་མཐོང་ན་དབང་ཐང་ཆེ། ཁྱུང་གི་དང་ག

པོ་སྲུགས་པས་མཐོང་ན་དྲག་པོའི་ལས

I will come there again to practice meditation." He made complimentary remarks such as these. This place, the upper route, is empowered from his visit.

This central mountain of the region, which sustains the area with many wondrous indications of spiritual attainment and manifestations of miraculous abilities from the visits of many other great beings such as that master among yogis gNyis-med rdo-rje, the leader of adepts Kun-dga' rgyal-mtshan, the great adept Thang-stong rgyal-po, great scholar/practitioner 'Jam-dbyangs grags-pa and so forth, rivals Mt Meru in its outward appearance to ordinary people. The very top of Gangs-dkar, with its crown of crystal, surpasses all other peaks in its brilliance. The outer form is extremely beautiful with its eight signs of good fortune[211] and seven auspicious royal symbols[212] and filled with all the various sorts of trees in the world and endless kinds of offerings such as parasols and flags. In the "neck" of the mountain is a great "banner" of light that appears by itself. As it changes color due to the sustaining power and total presence of the Awakened Ones of the three times, and you can see this right away, this is a sign that karmic obscurations are decreasing. If you are not yet able to perceive these phenomena, this is a sign that there are still some karmic and emotional afflictions. It is important to pay respect and recite the hundred syllables (mantra) and so on.

Also, if you see white, this is a sign that you will achieve a peaceful karma, a long-life, free of illness. Later you will be born in the Pure Land.

If you see yellow, you will realize a very expansive karma with much merit and a very comfortable life-style.

If you see red, you will have great power.

If you see green or dark (black) mantras this is a sign of intense karma.

འགྲུབ་ཅིང་གནས་ཀྱིས་སྟུང་བཟློག་སོགས་ལ་འབད་དགོས་པར་གསུངས། ཕྱི་ལྟར་ན་
སྣང་ངོར་ཤེལ་དང་མུ་ཏིག་སོགས་རིན་པོ་ཆེ་སྣ་ཚོགས་ལས་གྲུབ་པའི་ཕོ་བྲང་བཞི་
བརྩེགས་ཀྱི་ནང་དུ་གནས་ཀྱི་སྣུང་མ་དགོ་བསྙེན་རྡོ་རྗེ་རྣོ་གྲོས་འཁོར་བཅས་ལྔའི་
དཔལ་འབྱོར་ཕུན་སུམ་ཚོགས་པས་གནས་ཤིང༌། ནང་ལྟར་ན་འཐབས་པའི་གནས་
བཅུན་ཆེན་པོ་ཡན་ལག་འབྱུང་འཁོར་དུ་བཙུམ་པ་སྟོང་དང་ལྟ་བཀྲས་བསྐོར་ཏེ་
བཤགས་པ་ལས་ཅན་གྱི་གང་ཟག་རྣམས་ཀྱིས་མཐོན་སུམ་དུ་མཇལ་ནུས་པ་དང༌།
གསང་བ་ལྟར་ན་དཔལ་འཁོར་ལོ་སྡོམ་པའི་དཀྱིལ་འཁོར་རྟེན་དང་བརྟེན་པར་བཅས་
པ་ཡོངས་སུ་རྫོགས་པའི་ཙེ་མོ་བཞིར་སྣང་བར་གྲུབ་ཕོག་ཀུན་དགའ་རྒྱལ་མཚན་གྱིས་
གསུངས་ལ། རྒྱ་བར་མཁའ་འགྲོ་ཚོགས་སུང་རྣམས་ན་ཕུན་ལྷར་འཐིབས་པ་སོགས་
མདོར་ན་འོག་མིན་མཁའ་ལ་སྤྱོད་པ་དང་རྣམ་དབྱེར་མེད་པ་གསང་སྔགས་ཀྱི་རྣལ་
འབྱོར་གྲུབ་པ་རྣམས་ཀྱིས་དགའ་པའི་གཟིགས་སྣང་དུ་གྲུབ་པས་དེ་ལྟ་བུའི་གནས་རེ་འདི་
ཉིད་དང་ལ་ཅན་རྣམས་ཀྱིས་མིག་གིས་མཐོང་བ་ཙམ་གྱིས་བསྐལ་པ་སྟོང་དུ་བསགས་
པའི་སྡིག་སྒྲིབ་དག་པར་གསུངས་ཤིང༌། རེ་དེའི་ཞོལ་དུ་གཡོན་ངོས་སུ་ཐག་པོའི་གནས་
ཞེས་གྲགས་པ་དེར་ཐག་པོའི་སྐུ་དང་སྐགས་ཐེང་ཕྱག་མཚན་རྣམས་རང་བྱོན་འབུར་དུ་
དོད་པ་དང༌། གཞན་ཡང་སངས་རྒྱས་སྟོང་རྩ་གཉིས། སྤྲུལ་བླ་བདེ་གཤེགས་བརྒྱུད་
སོགས་ཀྱི་སྣུང་བཀུན་དང་གྲུབ་ཐགས་མང་དུ་ཡོད་ཀུང་དང་མེད་ལོག་ལྷ་ཅན་རྣམས་ཀྱི་
སྟོང་ཡུལ་མ་ཡིན་པར་གསུངས་ཤིང༌། གནས་དེའི་གཡས་ངོས་མདུན་རི་བོར་སྐྱོལ་མའི་
གནས་ཞེས་གྲགས་པར་སྐྱོལ་མ་ཉེར་གཅིག་དང༌། མ་གཅིག་ལབ་སྒྲོན་སོགས་གཅོད་
ཡུལ་བཀུད་པ་དང༌། བྱ་མ་སར་གྱི་སྐྲོ་ང་དང༌།

It is said that you will have to make efforts at averting this through other means of protection.

[86] As to the outer manifestation, the guardian deity dGe snyen rDo-rje blo-gros, together with his retinue, with all the most excellent wealth of the gods, lives in the middle of a four-storey palace that has been built of a variety of jewels, crystal and pearls. Inwardly, 'Phags-pa'i gnas-brtan chen-po lives together with 1500 saints (*arhants*).[213] Those with the karma can see them very clearly. Secretly, dPal 'Khor-lo sdom-pa (Cakrasamvara) together with the mandala and everything built on it is complete, appearing on the four peaks of the mountain, so the siddha Kun-dga' rgyal-mtshan has said.[214]

At the base (of the mountain) the dakinis and female protectors surround (envelope) the area like fog (making it appear to be obscured in darkness). In short, those whose accomplishments in the yoga of the "secret mantra" are inseparable in quality with experience of spaciousness of pure realms ('og-min mkha), are able to perceive what presents itself as pure vision. For those who have confidence in the mountain in this way, by merely seeing the mountain it is said that obscurations accumulated through negative activity over a thousand eons are purified.

The left face at the bottom of the mountain is known as Vajrayogini's place. There the image (sku) of Vajrayogini, mantra strings, symbolic representations that have appeared by themselves, jut out. There are also many signs (marks, indicators) or realization – images (snang brnyan) of the eight medicine Buddhas, 1002 awakened ones and so forth. It is said that this is not a place for those with wrong views or lacking in confidence. The area to the right of that place, in front of the mountain, is known as Tara's place. The letters of the vowels and consonants, a garuda egg, images of the gCod lineage, Ma-gcig lab-sgron and

དབུངས་གསལ་གྱི་ཡིག་འབྲུ་སོགས་ཕྲུག་ལས་རང་བྱོན་དང་། གྲུབ་ཆེན་བརྒྱད་ཅུ་རྩེ།
འཕགས་ནེར་ལྔ་ལྔ་ལྔང་དཔལ་རྡོར་ཀུམྦ་ལ་སོགས་སྙེས་མཆོག་མང་པོའི་གྲུབ་རྟགས་ཀྱི
ཕྱག་ཞབས་ཀྱི་རྗེས་དང་སྐུ་རྗེས་སོགས་གྲངས་མེད་པ་བཞུགས་ཤིང་། ཁྱད་པར་དབུས་
ཀྱིས་རི་བོ་རྗེ་བཙུན་སྒྲོལ་མའི་སྤུང་བརྩན་ཞིན་ཏུ་གསལ་ཞིང་རྒྱུན་ཆས་ཡོངས་སུ་
རྗོགས་པའི་ཕྱགས་ཀའི་ཐད་དང་གསང་བ་ཕྱགས་ཀྱི་སྤུབས་ཞེས་གྲགས་གནས་སྟོ་ཁྱང་
པར་དུ་འཕགས་པ་ཡོད་ཅིང་རི་བོ་པོ་ཏ་ལ་དང་གཡུ་ལོ་བཀོད་པའི་ཞིང་གི་ཡོན་ཏན་དང་
ཁྱད་པར་མེད་པར་གསུངས་ལས་ཕྱག་མཆོད་གསོལ་འདེབས་ལ་འབད་ན་གནས་
སྐབས་དུས་མི་འཆི་བ་སོགས་འདིགས་པ་མཐའ་དག་ལས་སྐྱོབ་ཅིང་མཐར་ཕྱག་རྗེ་
བཙུན་འཕགས་མ་ཉེས་པར་རྗེས་སུ་བཟུང་བར་འགྱུར་ལ། གནན་ཡང་འཕགས་མོའི
གནས་ཀྱི་གཡས་ཟུར་དུ་སེང་གདོང་མའི་གནས་དང་། ལས་མགོན་བྱུ་རོག་གདོང་ཅན
གྱི་རང་བྱོན་དང་། དཔའ་བོ་དཔའ་མོ་རྣམས་ཆོགས་འཁོར་འདུ་བའི་གནས་དེ་བཞང་གི
དད་པ་འཕུལ་བ་དང་། ཆོས་འབྱུང་གི་དཀྱིལ་དུ་མཁས་གྲུབ་འཛམ་དབྱངས་གྲགས
པས་གནས་དང་གཞི་བདག་ལ་ཁྲུས་གསོལ་སོགས་མཛད་པའི་བཞུགས་ཁྲི་མི་མ་ཡིན
རྣམས་ཀྱིས་བཀྱིགས་པ་ཡོད་ཅིང་། དེ་གཡོན་ཕྱོགས་རྗེ་སྒྱིལ་ཕན་ཆུན་དུ་ཀུམྦ་ཏོལ
པའི་རྡོ་རྗེ་དང་། གྲུབ་ཐོབ་ཀུན་དགའ་རྒྱལ་མཆན་གཞིས་ཀྱི་ཆོས་ཁྲི་རེ་རེ་དང་། གྲུབ
ཐོབ་ཀུན་དགའ་རྒྱལ་མཆན་གྱིས་བཏོན་པའི་གྲུབ་པའི་རྒྱ་མིག་ཡོད་ལ། དེ་ནས་ཕྱིན་པ
ལ་སྐུ་གསུང་ཕྱགས་ཀྱི་ལྷ་མོ་རེ་མ་ཏི་དང་རེ་མ་ཛ་རེ་མ་ཌ་གསུམ་ཀྱི་བླ་མཆོ་གཡུ་མཆོ
སྤུན་གསུམ་ཆར་དུ་དངར་བ་དང་། གནན་ཡང་ཁ་དོག་མི་འདུ་བའི་མཆོ་ཕུན་མང་དུ
ཡོད་པ་རྣམས་ནི་སྤྱལ་དང་ཡང་སྤྱལ་གྱི་ལྷ་མོ་རྣམས་ཀྱི

so forth and the twenty-one Tara's have appeared by themselves out of the rock.

[87]. There are numerous imprints of the body, feet or hands, signs of realization of many excellent, outstanding people such as the Karmapa, Lha-lung dpal-rdo, 84 mahasiddhas, Guru Rinpoche and his 25 disciples. Particularly in the middle part of the mountain is a very clear image, ornamented completely in the area of the heart, of venerable Tara known as the gSang-ba thugs-kyi sgrub ("Realization of a Mysterious Response"). This place is regarded as especially sacred. It is said that there is no difference between Ri-po-ta-la[215] and the capabilities inherent in [this place called] gYu-lo bkod-pa'i zhing. If you are diligent is diligent in paying respects and prayers, it is said that you will be protected from all anxiety and situations such as an untimely death and so forth. You will be looked after for sure by the venerable Holy Lady. Also, off to the right of Tara's place is Seng gdong-ma's niche and that of Las-mgon with the face of a crow. Both of these have appeared by themselves. This is a place where groups of powerful male and female spirits gather. Very pleasant odors and scents come out from here. In the center is a triangular area where the scholar/practitioner 'Jam-dbyangs grags-pa made prayers and oblations to the local spirits (gzhi bdag). There is also a throne built by non-humans. To the left of that area, here and there both the Karmapa Rol-pa'i rdo-rje and the siddha Kun-dga' rgyal-mtshan had stone huts with thatched roofs with a "dharma throne" (chos khri). There is a spring that was made to come forth by the siddha Kun-dga' rgyal-mtshan. Then, past that is a row of three lakes: bLa mtsho, g'Yu mtsho, sPun-mtsho for the three goddesses as pattern, communication, and response, Ramati, Ramadza, and Ramadzu respectively. There are also lots of little lakes of different colors. These are said to be the abodes of the goddesses associated with incarnation and reincarnation.

གནས་ཡིན་པར་གསུངས། དེ་ནས་མར་ཕྱིན་པས་བྲག་དང་རྒྱ་མཚམས་ཀྱི་དུར་ཁྲོད་དུ་
ཕྱག་མོ་གྲུ་འདྲལ་ནག་མོའི་རང་བྱུང་དང་། གནན་ཡང་ཞི་དང་ཁྲོ་བོའི་ལྷ་སྐུ་དང་ཕྱག་
མཚན་ཡིག་འབྲུ་དུ་མའི་རང་བྱོན་ཡོད་ཅིང་དེར་ཕྱག་མཆོད་གསོལ་འདེབས་རྗེ་གཅིག་
ཏུ་བྱས་ནས་གྲུ་གཉེན་ས་བདག་གི་གདོན་ཐམས་ཅད་བྱང་བར་འགྱུར་ལ། དེ་ནས་རེ་
ཉེད་དུ་ཡར་ཕྱིན་པས་མི་ཤག་མཁས་པ་མི་ལྕེའི་ཡ་གྱལ་འཕགས་པ་སྤུན་རས་གཟིགས་
ཀྱི་རྣམ་འཕྲུལ་མཚུངས་མེད་བྱམས་སར་བ་ཡེ་ཤེས་དཔལ་གྱི་སྐུབ་གནས་དང་། རྡོ་ལ་
ཕྱག་གིས་ལ་འཇུའི་ཡིག་དྲུག་བྲིས་པ་སོགས་བཞུགས་པའི་གདུང་འབུམ་ལ་དུས་བཟང་
རྣམས་སུ་འཛའ་འོད་མེ་ཏོག་གི་ཆར་པ་སོགས་ཀུན་གྱིས་མཐོང་བའི་མཆོད་རྟེན་ཅེས་
ཁྱད་པར་དུ་འཕགས་པ་དང་། དེ་ནས་ཅུང་ཟད་ཡར་ཕྱིན་པས་རབ་སྐྱང་གི་གྲུབ་ཐོབ་
རྣམ་གསུམ་གྱི་ཡ་གྱལ་དཔལ་ལ་ར་ཆོས་རྗེ་ཉི་མ་རྒྱལ་མཚན་གྱིས་བསྙེན་སྒྲུབ་མཛད་
སྐྱབས་ཀྱི་བཞུགས་གནས་ཡོད་ཅིང་། དེ་ནས་མར་ཕྱིན་པས་དམ་ཅན་གཡས་མཁར་
འགྲམ་དུ་སློན་དམ་ཆིག་ཉམས་པ་ཞིག་གིས་རྒྱུན་བྱས་ནས་གཡུ་སྒྲོན་མས་གནས་
བསྟིལ་ཏེ་བུ་འོད་ཆེན་པོ་བྱུང་བའི་ཚེ་གྲུབ་ཐོབ་ཀུན་དགའ་རྒྱལ་མཚན་གྱིས་དུ་བསྲིག་
མཛད་ནས་གཏོར་སློད་དང་སྐུ་ཚེས་བཟབས་པའི་རྗེས་དང་། དུང་དཀར་ཁ་སློད་ཀྱི་རང་
བྱོན། དེ་འོག་ཞིག་པོ་གཉིས་མེད་རྡོ་རྗེའི་ཆིབས་གཡག་གི་ཞབས་རྗེས་དང་། མགོན་པོ་
སྔག་ཞོན་གྱི་ཆིབས་སྔག་གི་རྗེས། དམ་ཅན་གྱི་ཆིབས་ར་དང་པོ་རྗེས་སོགས་ཡོད་ཅིང་།
གྱིང་ནང་གི་ཆུ་མིག་ནི་གྲུབ་ཐོབ་ཀུན་དགའ་རྒྱལ་མཆན་གྱིས་གྲུབ་རྒྱ་བཏོན་པ་ཡིན་ལ།
གྱིང་འོག་ཏུ་གྲུབ་པའི་དབང་མོ་དགེ་བའི་སློལ་མའི་ལྷ་གའི་རྗེས་དང་། གྲུབ་ཐོབ་ཆེན་
པོའི་གསང་རྫོར་རྗེས་སོགས་ཡོད་ཅིང་། ལས་

[88] Then, going down, is a burial site of rock and water (shed), and a self-appearing Phag-mo khu-'dul nag-mo. There are many self-appearing letters and marks of hands and "bodies" of peaceful and wrathful deities. If you pay homage and make prayers with focused attention, all harm that comes from spirits of the water (klu), mountain spirits (gnyan), and "rulers of the land" (sa bdag) is purified. Then, going farther up the middle of the mountain is the retreat place of one of the five Minyak scholars, Byams-sar-ba Ye-shes dpal, incomparable emanation of Avalokitesvara. He wrote lantsa letters with his hand in the rock. In good times for thousands of generations it has existed, and this place is more special than a great mchod-rten (stupa) from which you could see everywhere, or rainbow light or a shower of flowers.

Then, if you go a little further up, there is the place where one of the three Rab-sgang sages, dPal A-ra chos-rje nyi-ma rgyal-mtshan, lived in retreat. Then, going down a bit, on the shore of the sacred fort on the right is where a turquoise-colored piece of the glacier broke off on account of conditions caused by not keeping commitments. When that happened a great flood came. The sage Kun-dga' rgyal-mtshan turned this flood away and, after bringing together offerings and images,[216] a white conch appeared by itself. Below there is a footprint left by gNyis-med rdo-rje when he rode a yak; one when mGon-po rode a tiger, and there are sacred stables and enclosures. The springs of the inner island were brought forth by the sage Kun-dga' rgyal-mtshan. At the lower island, there is an impression of the labia of dGe-ba'i sgrol-ma, the great female adept, and markings left by gSang-ba rdo-rje, the great *siddha*.

95

སྐྱོབ་དགའ་བྱེད་ཀྱི་རྒྱུ་མིག་དང་། དྲང་དཀར་རབ་བྱོན། སྐྱིད་དུ་ཡར་སྐྱེབས་ལ་ཁད་ཀྱི་
སྒྱུང་སྦྱོངས་གོང་དུ་བྱུབ་ཆེན་ཐབ་སྦོང་རྒྱལ་པོས་རྗེ་ཕ་བོང་གི་སྟེང་དུ་འཁྱུལ་འབོར་
མཛད་པའི་སྐུ་རྗེས་རྣམས་ཡོད། དེ་ནས་མར་ཕྱིན་པས་དམ་སྲིད་སྐྱུན་དགུ་དུས་སླབ་
དབྱིབས་ཀྱི་ཕ་བོང་གི་ཞབས་སུ་མནན་པ་དེ་ལ་གཡས་གཡོན་དགུ་དགུ་བསྐོར་ཞིང་
དམོད་བྱས་ན་དམ་སྲི་འབྱུང་པོའི་བར་ཆད་ཀྱིས་མི་ཚུགས་པར་འགྱུར་ལ། དེ་འོག་སྒྲུབ་
ཐོབ་ཀུན་དགའ་རྒྱལ་མཚན་རྒྱ་ཡུལ་ཞེབས་པའི་དུས་སུ་བར་ཆད་བརློག་རྟགས་ཀྱི་
ཞབས་རྗེས་དང་། འཇུ་རུ་དཔོན་པོའི་གསོལ་མཛོ་འི་རྗེས་དང་།ཁ་བོང་བཞགས་པའི་
སྟ་རེ་རུག་རྗེས་དང་། གཟིམས་དྲེལ་འཁྲབ་པའི་རྗེས་དང་། ཡིག་འབྲུ་ཕྱག་མཚན་
སོགས་རང་བྱོན་མང་དུ་ཡོད་ཅིང་། དེ་ནས་མར་ཕྱིན་པས་བྱུབ་ཐོབ་ཀུན་དགའ་རྒྱལ་
མཚན་གྱིས་བོན་པོའི་བྱད་བརློག་གི་ཚོར་འཕངས་པའི་གཏོར་མ་སྟོང་དང་བཅས་པ་
དང་ཚེས་གོས་བཟབས་པའི་གྲུ་རྗེས་ཤིན་ཏུ་གསལ་བ་དང་། རྗེ་ཙ་འི་གདོན་བསྐྲལ་བའི་
རྟ་མགོ་དུ་མ་བུ་གཞིས་དང་ས་བདག་བསྐྲལ་བའི་ཕག་མགོའི་དུ་མ་རྐྱམས་ཡོད་ལ། དེ་
ནས་རྒྱབ་རིའི་སྟེ་མོར་སྐྱེབས་པའི་སྲུམ་མདོའི་གོང་དུ་མི་འཁྲུགས་པའི་གནས་མཆལ་རྒྱུ་
ཡོད་ཅིང་དང་མོས་རྩེ་གཅིག་པས་ཕྱག་བསྐོར་བྱས་ན་ལས་སྒྲིབ་སྦྱོང་ནས་པར་གསུངས་
ཤིང་། དགོན་ནང་གི་རྟེན་གྱི་གཙོ་བོ་འི་ཐམས་ཅད་མཁྱེན་པ་ཀླུ་རོལ་པའི་རྗེ་རྗེ་དེ་
ཉིད་རྒྱ་ནག་གོང་མ་རོར་ཀྱི་རྒྱལ་པོ་ཐོ་གན་ཐེ་མུར་གྱིས་ཨོ་བྱང་ཆེན་པོར་སྐྱན་དུངས་
ནས་ཡར་ཕེབས་པའི་ཚེ་རྒྱ་ནག་ལོ་བྱང་ཉིད་ནས་གདན་དྲངས་ཏེ་དགོན་འདིའི་རྟེན་
སྐལ་དུ་གནང་བའི་ཇོ་བོ་གསུང་བྱོན་མ་ཤིན་ཏུ་བྱིན་ཆེན་དང་། མཁའ་འགྲོ་མ་བྱེ་བ་
དཀོས་སུ་ཐིམ་པའི་གུ་རུའི་སྐུ་འདྲ་མེ་

[89] There is also a spring that purifies obscurations, a white conch that appeared by itself, and as one gradually goes above the islands (temples), before a grassy valley is a boulder with markings left by the siddha Thang-stong rgyal-po, made during 'khrul-'khor practice. Then, lower down, nine kindred harmful spirits [dam-srid spun-dgu] have been put down under the base of a rock shaped like a turtle. These nine relatives encircle to the right and left, but if you should utter an oath, obstacles thrown up by demonic forces opposed to spiritual practice will not be able to harm you. Below there the siddha Kun-dga' rgyal-mtshan left a foot print as a mark of overcoming obstructions when he was going to China. There is a hoof print of a female mdzo as it was being led by its master, an impression of an axe left when it struck a rock, and there are many letters, hand prints that appeared by themselves, and a hoof print of a mule.

Then, going lower down the impressions of the siddha Kun-dga' rgyal-mtshan's robes and the container of the "throwing the sickle" offering used in turning back the spells of a Bon-po are very clear. There are also parts of a pig's head to indicate liberation of masters of the land (sa-bdag) and two parts of a horse head to indicate the liberation from the harm made by dri-za. Then, as you reach the end of the back of the mountain before Sum-mdo you will come upon an undisturbed place. If you pays your respects with single-minded devotion it is said that you be able to purify obstructions caused by your actions (karma).

The main statue in the monastery is one of the "completely sensitive" Karma-pa Rol-pa'i rdo-rje. An earlier emperor of China, the Mongolian King Tho-gan the-mun, had invited him to the palace; when the Karmapa came to this monastery, having been invited there from the Chinese palace, he gave this statue as an image possessing good fortune for the monastery. It is known as the mirror image of the guru's form, with ten million dakinis dissolved into it, an image that speaks and filled with great sustaining power.

ལོང་མ་ཞེས་གྲགས་པ་དང་། དཔལ་ཀུ་རུ་བ་རང་བྱུང་རྡོ་རྗེའི་སྐུ་འདྲ་གྲོལ་བའི་བཞི་ལྷུན་
ཤིན་ཏུ་ཁྱུད་འཕགས་གསེར་ཟངས་ལས་གྲུབ་པ་དང་། གྲུབ་ཐོབ་ལ་ར་ཚོས་རྗེ་དམ་
ཅན་འཕོར་བཅས་དངོས་སུ་བསྒྲིམས་པའི་རྡོ་རྗེ་ལེགས་པའི་སྐུ་བརྙན་གྱི་མཐུ་དྲག་ཅུ་ལ་
རྡོ་སྦྱུར་ཤིན་ཏུ་ཆེ་བ་སོགས་བཞུགས་པ་སྟེ་དེ་དག་ནི་གནས་རྟེན་གྱི་བཞུགས་ཚུལ་མདོ་
ཚམ་སྨོས་པ་ཡིན་ལ། གཞན་ཡང་མཐའ་བསྐོར་ལམ་བར་གྱི་གནས་སོགས་རྒྱས་པར་
གནས་ཡིག་ལྟ་མ་རྣམས་ལས་རྟོགས་པར་བྱའོ། །

གཉིས་པ་གནས་འདུས་སྐབས་ཀྱི་ཕན་ཡོན་བྱེ་བྲག་ཏུ་བཤད་པ་ནི། དེ་ལྟར་གོང་དུ་རྗེ་
སྐད་བཤད་པའི་གནས་དང་རྟེན་དེ་དག་ལས་ལོག་ལྟ་དང་ཁྱད་གསོད་ཀྱིས་བརྐུས་
བཙོས་དང་རྗེ་མི་སྐྲ་དུ་འཛིན་པ་སོགས་སྟེག་དང་འདྲེས་པའི་བསམ་སྦྱོར་ཐམས་ཅད་
སྤང་སྟེ། དང་འདོད་ཡིད་ཆེས་ཀྱི་དད་པ་ཅེ་གཅིག་གུན་ནས་བསྐྱེད་དེ་ཕྱག་མཆོད་
བསྐོར་བ་སོགས་བྱས་ན་དུས་ནམ་དུའང་གནས་གཞན་དུ་བྱས་པ་བས་དགེ་རྩའི་ཕན་
ཡོན་གྱི་འགྱུར་སྟོབས་ཆེ་ཞིང་ལྷག་པར་རྐྱང་ལོ་ནས་ཧར་གྱི་གནས་འདུས་སྐབས་སུ་
འོག་མིན་དག་པ་མཁའ་སྤྱོད་ཀྱི་ཞིང་དང་། ཐུབ་ཕྱོགས་ཨོ་རྒྱན་གྱི་ཡུལ་དཔལ་ཚ་རི་ཏུ་
སོགས་གནས་ཡུལ་གཞན་གྱི་དཔར་བོ་མཁའ་འགྲོ་དགྲ་ཅན་སྲུང་མ་དང་བཅས་པ་
འདིར་འདུས་ཤིང་། རྩ་གསུམ་ལྷ་ཚོགས་ཐམས་ཅད་སྐུ་གསུང་ཐུགས་ཀྱི་བྱིན་རླབས་མ་
ལུས་གནས་འདིར་ཐབ་པས། རྟོགས་པ་མཆོག་ཐོབ་པའི་རྩལ་འབྱོར་ཅན་རྣམས་ལ་
དག་པའི་གཟིགས་སྣང་འབྱམས་ཀླས་པ་སྣང་བ་སྟོས་ཆེ་དགོས་དེ་ཉུང་ཟད་ལས་དག་པ་
རྣམས་ཀྱི་སྣང་ངོར་ཡང་། ལྷ་སྒྲ། ཕྱག་མཆན། ཡིག་འབྲུ། འཇའ་འོད་ཐིག་ལེ་བསང་
དུད་ཀྱི་རྣམ་པ་སོགས་མཐོང་སྣང་མི་འདྲ་བ

[90] The likeness of Karmapa Rang-byung rdo-rje is imbued with four liberating qualities[217] and is very special in being made from a golden-colored copper. There is an image of rDo-rje legs-pa into which the *siddha* A-ra chos-rje dissolved the guardians and their retinues with a strong, fiercely-creative, quick and clear energy. This is just a brief mention of these sacred places. Also the (descriptions of) places on the trails in the surrounding area are taken from more detailed guide books (gnas yig) written at earlier times.

Second is the explanation on the specific benefits that are present there (gnas 'dus). When your are near these images or places described above, you must abandon (give up) all negative thinking in which you do not care about the consequences of your actions, especially wrong views and bringing harm through killing. You should give rise to wanting, trusting, longing confidence with complete attention when you take refuge, make offerings, circumambulate. The benefit in fundamental positive qualities from what has been done in another place or time will become stronger, especially in the Ox year in which there is a great gathering in the East. The sacred guardians, *dakinis, dakas* of other regions such as Orgyan, glorious Tsaritra and so on, from dynamic fields of pure practice such as 'Og-min, gather there. Since all the sustaining power in the existential, communicative, and responsive functions of the three roots and all the hosts of divine energies is gathered here, for those who have linked with Being's source and have come to a most excellent realization, everything is seen as pure. Whatever presents itself, the different patterns that can appear in the form of incense smoke, spots, rainbow light, written letters, marks of hands (impressions of hands), images of deities, even the most subtle phenomena such as a song, musical notes of stringed instruments, whatever one might hear,

དང་། སྒྱུ་གར་དང་། པི་ཝཾ། རོལ་མོའི་སྒྲ་སྙན་པ་སོགས་ཐོས་པ་དང་། སྨོས་དུང་
སོགས་དྲི་ཞིམ་པོའི་རིགས་ཚོར་བ་དང་། སྤྱི་ལམ་དུ་དགའ་བའི་སྐྱང་བ་དང་། མཁའ་
འགྲོའི་ཡུལ་བསྟན་སོགས་འབྱུང་བར་གསུངས་ལ། དེའི་ཚེ་གནས་འདིར་ཞག་བདུན་
བསྟེན་སྒྲུབ་བྱས་ན་གཞན་དུ་ལོ་བདུན་ནས་ཚེ་གཅིག་ལ་སྒྲུབ་པ་བྱས་པ་དང་བསོད་
ནམས་མཉམ་ཞིང་། བསྐོར་བ་གཅིག་བྱས་ན་མ་ཧེ་ཏུང་ཕྱུར་བརྒྱ་འདོན་པའི་ཕན་ཡོན་
དང་། མཐའ་བསྐོར་གཅིག་བྱས་ན་ཕྱབ་དབང་བཞུགས་གནས་བརྒྱུད་དང་། པདྨའི་
སྐྱབ་གནས་བརྒྱ་རྩ་བསྐོར་བའི་ཕན་ཡོན་དང་མཚུངས་ཞིང་། ཚོགས་མཆོད་ཕུལ་བས་
ཚོགས་གཉིས་ཀྱི་བར་མཐོང་འགོངས། མར་མེ་འབུལ་བས་མ་རིག་པའི་སྨུན་པ་སེལ་
ཞིང་ཡེ་ཤེས་ཀྱི་སྣང་བ་རྒྱས། ཕྱག་གཅིག་འཚལ་བས་ཀུང་བསྐལ་པ་མང་པོའི་སྡིག་
སྒྲིབ་དག། རོ་དང་དང་བཀླས་བརྗོད་སོགས་གང་བྱས་འབུམ་ཕྲག་མང་པོར་འགྱུར་
བས། ཐམས་ཅད་ཀྱིས་ཕྱག་མཆོད་བསྐོར་བ་གསོལ་འདེབས་སོགས་རྣམ་དཀར་གྱི་
དགེ་རྩ་ཆེ་ཕྱལ་འབད་ན་སྒྱིག་ཅན་ཁན་པ་སོགས་ཀྱང་ན་སོད་དུ་མི་ལྡང་ཞིང་མཐོ་
རིས་ཐོབ་པ་དང་། ཚེ་འདིར་ལས་ཉོན་སྒྱིག་སྒྲིབ་བར་ཆད་ཐམས་ཅད་བྱང་ཞིང
བསྒྲུབས་པས་ཚེ་རིང་ཞིང་ནད་མེད་པ་དང་། བསོད་ནམས་དང་ལོངས་སྤྱོད་ཀྱི་འབྱོར
པ་ཐོབ་ཅིང་། སྨོན་ལམ་གང་བཏབ་འགྲུབ་པ་དང་དམ་པའི་ཆོས་སྒྲུབ་པའི་སྐལ
བ་ཅན་དུ་འགྱུར་ཞིང་། ཕྱི་མ་བདེ་བ་ཅན་སོགས་དག་པའི་ཞིང་རྣམས་སུ་སྐྱེ་ཞིང་གནས
འདིར་འགྲོལ་ཚད་ཐམས་ཅད་རིང་པོར་མི་ཐོགས་པར་བླ་མེད་བྱང་ཆུབ་ཀྱི་གོ་འཕང
ཐོབ་པར་སྐྱོབ་དཔོན་རིན་པོ་ཆེ་པདྨ་སཾ་བྷ་བའི་བསྒྲུ་མེད་རྡོ་རྗེའི་ཡུང་ལས་ཡང་ཡང
བཀའ་སྩལ་འདུག་པས་སྐྱོ་ཐམས་ཅད

pleasant sensations of sweet-smelling incense, the unfolding of feelings of purity in dreams, and the dakinis that are said to appear with prophecies, are just the manifesting of purity. At that time, if you practice for seven days the merit is the same as practicing for 7 years at some other stretch of time. If you carry out one circumambulation, this has the same benefit as reciting a hundred-million manis. If you make an outer-circumambulation (thub dbang bzhugs gnas brgyad), this is the same benefit as circumambulating the Lotus Born's hundred practice places. By making offerings you fill the treasure of the two accumulations. By offering butter lamps, the darkness of unknowing is dispelled and the unfolding of pristine cognition is expanded. By making homage once, the negativity (accumulated) over many eons is purified. If you recite the *jo-dar* the effects are multiplied hundreds of thousands of times. If you make efforts large or small in wholesome, white-root actions - with total commitment in prostrations, offerings, circumambulation, prayers and so forth, the suffering that comes from having obstructions will not lead you to lower states of existence. You will achieve a heavenly existence. Here, in this life, actions, conflicting emotions, obscurations and obstacles - all are purified. Having all of this come to you, you will have a long life, no sickness and a comfortable life-style from having made a connection with what is meritorious. You will become a fortunate person who is able to practice the sacred "dharma" and achieve whatever you wish for. Later you will be born in a pure place such as the Pure Land and so forth. Everything connected with this place, as it has been talked about again and again in the honest, enduring traditions of the Precious Teacher Padmasambhava, in quickly attaining the citadel of incomparable pure totality, from every channel great waves of merit and pristine

ནས་བསྲོད་ནམས་དང་ཡེ་ཤེས་ཀྱི་ཚོགས་རྒྱ་བས་པོ་ཆེ་འབད་པས་མཐོན་པར་འདུ་བགྱི་བའི་སློ་ནས་དཔའ་བའི་རྟེན་བཟང་ལས་སྐྱིད་པོ་ལེན་པར་མཛད་འཚལ། མཛད་ལོ། །

[92] awareness is gathered clearly because of these efforts. With a good foundation of leisure, please take this to heart, and accept its main meaning.

Mangalam.

Appendix A

The biography of the one called Bo Gangkar Rinpoche, "Precious White Glacier Mountain Incarnation," reflects the tremendous changes to the lives of people in Kham, the name given to parts of western Sichuan, Gansu, and Qinghai, through which the Yangtse (Jinsha), Mekong (Lancang), Salween (Nu), Yalong[218] rivers flow. They are culturally Tibetan and live in the regions that make up the watersheds of these great rivers. Those who live in Kham call themselves Khampas. The part of Kham inhabited by the Minyak is known as Kham-Minyak.

The massive peak known to the Chinese as Gonga Shan rests at the end of the Da Xue Shan (Great Snowy Mountains) range which stretches north to south across several autonomous regions in western Sichuan. The Chinese name for the peak, Gonga, is derived from the Tibetan/Minyak name Bo Gangkar, or "White Glacier Mountain." Much of the area around this mountain, particularly on the west and north sides, is now a nature preserve. The mountain has long been regarded as sacred by those living in its vicinity and its surrounding valleys and plateaus have a much-deserved reputation as an ideal environment for meditation and the cultivation of spiritual practice. It is also where many herbs used in Tibetan and Chinese medicine can be found. The villagers, high pasture yak herders, woodsmen, farmers who live in the valleys below the glaciers call themselves Minyakpa.[219]

Kham-Minyak[220]

Information available in English on the history of the Kham region of China is limited at present.[221] Even less has been written about Minyak. What follows is a compilation of information from Tibetan sources, scholarly journals, books by early explorers in Kham and political officers who traveled or lived in Eastern Tibet in the late 19th to mid-20th centuries. It is by no means complete. Events in the complex history of Kham during the last 150 years are open to a wide range of interpretation. In order to properly unravel the full story, a modern history of Kham will rely on interviews with surviving individuals from all walks of life who have witnessed life in Kham in the early 20th century and certainly make use of sources available at libraries in Britain, the United States, and China.

Originally the Minyak people are counted as one of the six clans of the Powo Dong tribe. Minyak Gonpo notes, "Minyak comprised the lGa, lDong and rMu tribes who came from six lineages of the Mi'u people, ancestors of the Tibetans. In the east were the rGya-nag (Chinese), the 'Jang in the south, the sTod-bod (Tibetans) in the west, and Sogs-po (Mongolians) in the North. In the middle of this region known as Greater Minyak was Minyak consisting of lower mDo, Gha, and Minyak, consisting of upper mDo and Kham Minyak."[222]

Who were the Minyak people in ancient Tibetan history? It is said by Minyak people in Kham that the area called Minyak was the original homeland of the Minyak people. At some period in the past which has yet to be determined from archaeological records, various clans, including the Minyak, moved north from the Shaluli and Daxue Shan regions of Kham-Minyak, and were known to other groups as the

Northern Dong or "Dongjang" (lDong-byang) in Tibetan. The spelling of this name using Wade-Giles transcription for Chinese is T'ang-hsiang. The second part of the Tibetan name for the lDong tribe, "byang" meaning north, is pronounced in central Tibetan dialect as "jang" with the "j" pronounced like in "jack." However, in some Kham dialects the letter ba with a subjoined ya, the bya syllable, is also pronounced like the French "ja" as in "Jacques". The Northern Dong tribe included the Minyak, the major group in the tribe, so to speak. Some say that the name Minyak was given to the northern branch of the lDong tribe later. The Byang-ga ("Northerners") called themselves both Minyak (and Mi for short).[223] From Byang-ga, pronounced Jangga with the J as in Jack, we get the Chinese name Qiang.

The Minyak word for silk cloth, "*tangkus*", became another name for the people as well, Tangut, the more familiar term in the West for the Minyak kingdom and people. Those who study the Xi Xia, or the Tangut, believe that the Minyak group in the lDong tribe came from present-day Sichuan.

"During the early decades of the T'ang dynasty, under constant attack by the expanding Tibetan empire, a *major portion of the Tang-hsiang migrated from Western Sichuan, their original homeland, to the area of the Great Bend of the Yellow River...* [italics mine] After the Huang Ch'ao rebellion (875-884), taking advantage of the general decline of the T'ang dynasty, the Tang-hsiang, and with them the entire Hsia prefecture, assumed full independence."[224] A semi-autonomous government had already been formed in and around the prefecture by then.

This independent group controlled the silk route where it passed through the Gansu corridor for 195 years "through four rulers in the Sung Dynasty starting in the first time cycle in the Water Monkey Year (1032) and lasting until the fourth time cycle in the Fire Pig Year (1227)."[225]

Additional dates for the Xi Xia (Minyak) kingdom have been given some stating the kingdom existed for 242 years from

1038-1280, with 1280 reflecting the continuation of the empire in Kara Khoto after the fall of the main capital in 1227, and more recently for 245 years from 982-1227. Most sources use the destruction of the Xi Xia capital in 1227 as the final year of the kingdom.

In 1006, the Minyak declared themselves independent, taking advantage of the political rivalry between the Liao people in the regions to the north, and the Song dynasty. After the capital was moved to Xingzhou, they had control over the Hexi corridor, the key section of the Silk Route leading from central China to the west.

The Minyak king declared himself equal to the Song emperor and by 1040 the Song were sending silk, silver, tea and other goods in annual tribute to the Minyak "Silk King". By the late 11th century Minyak territorial control extended to Dunhuang. An important site for the Minyak kingdom was at Kara Khoto, a place mentioned by Marco Polo. It became the destination of surviving members of the kingdom fleeing Genghis Khan's armies which destroyed the kingdom in 1227. Minyak tradition has it that Genghis Khan was killed by the Minyak queen following the final battle at the Minyak capital. Kara Khoto eventually was swallowed by the sands of the Gobi desert years after permanent drought forced it to be abandoned.

Genghis Khan's armies followed what these days would be called a "scorched earth policy". This meant burning houses, crops, killing all males, and taking females as slaves. It has been said that after the Mongolian troops left an area there was no building left standing, no animal or male human left alive. When the Minyak kingdom was destroyed, its culture and people were practically wiped out. Remnants of the kingdom moved to Kara Khoto as mentioned. Descendents of the royal household gradually moved back to the traditional homeland near present-day Kangding in Sichuan and re-established the kingdom at Dartsendo.

After the reign of Langdarma, from the 9th to 11th centuries Buddhist teachings were in decline in central Tibet. However, Buddhist teachings thrived in Minyak monasteries. Minyak scholars were traveling to India, some even settling there and adopting Indian names. Minyak scholars were living at Nalendra, the seat of Buddhist learning in India, when Atisa was there before he was invited to Tibet in the late 11th century. When the Mongolians invaded Tibet and appointed the Sakya family rulers of the territory, the translator for the Sakya ruler and the Mongolian king was from Minyak.

The infrastructure of monasteries and routes for travel between India and Minyak was maintained despite repeated invasions by the Mongolians. Destroyed monasteries were rebuilt and some out-of-the-way temples built by followers of Padmasambhava were spared destruction due to their remoteness; some 10th century Minyak monasteries still remain.[226] Legend has it that Guru Rinpoche and his students left Central Tibet, passed through Minyak before they settled in northern Kham. Since then Minyak has been a special place for followers of Guru Rinpoche. There is also a strong connection with Minyak because one of Guru Rinpoche's principle teachers, Sri Singha, came from the Minyak region.

In the 7th century, the Tibetan ruler Srong-btsan sgam-po built a series of temples across what is now mostly the Tibetan Autonomous Region. The eastern-most temple, situated 105km west of Kangding, was built at Minyak rab-sgang or Minyak ring-mo. That was the name of the area in the 7th century, recorded in the life history of Srong-brtsan sgam- po and elsewhere. It is now known as Lha-gang. That places the Minyakpa at the middle of what they have considered Mi-nyag approximately 400 years before the Xi Xia kingdom.

After the Zhangga or Minyakpa took over what are now Qinghai, Gansu, and parts of Sichuan, members of the ruling family moved to the west over time. Current research[227] shows influences of the Minyakpa on the Bhutanese royal lineages and on central Tibetan politics at the time of the early Sakya rulers. Equally exciting is the work on the language of Zhang-zhung, the ancient kingdom in Western Tibet which suggests that Zhang-zhung is a variant of Minyak.[228] Since evidence suggests that the Tibetan system of writing was modeled on that used in Zhang-zhung, there is some speculation that one early system of writing for the Minyakpa may have been similar to Tibetan cursive style.

Kham has been settled for a long time, with local legends claiming the area as the original homeland of the Tibetans as well. The regions Tibetans inhabit can be differentiated into a political area controlled by the central Tibetan government and an ethnographic area outside the political controls of a single governing body, but culturally Tibetan. The Tibetan Autonomous Region today falls within the traditional areas in which the central Tibetan government was able to maintain some form of direct political control. Kham, roughly half of present-day western Sichuan, Qinghai and Gansu, comprising large parts of what are known as Amdo in Tibetan, and sections of northern Yunnan (Muli, Minyak) are areas in the ethnographic area of Tibet. Historically these regions were largely outside the direct political control of the central Tibetan government and by tradition under the leadership of tribal leaders, warlords or local "kings" (such as at Dege and Minyak). The political area is called Tibet and the predominantly ethnographically-Tibetan regions called specifically either Kham or Amdo.

Some in the Tibetan government in exile have claimed that the Sino-Tibetan treaty of 783 gave the territory of Kham to the central Tibetan government. For the next thousand years or so following the treaty, Tibetan culture dominated the Kham area though the central Tibetan

government had little authority. The influence of Minyak was very strong and widespread. The ruling Tibetan government would eventually favor the Gelukpa Buddhist sect from the early 15th century onwards but this school did not establish as strong a presence, in terms of number of monasteries, in Kham as it did in Amdo to the north, or Tibet itself.

Kham was largely under the control of the King of Chala and other autonomous principalities such as at Dege in the 600 years following the collapse of the Minyak (Xi Xia) kingdom in 1227, and the migration of the Minyak tribe. The Chala King lived at eastern Kham's major town of Kangding or Dardo. One of the other large Kham principalities was Dege to the northwest of Kangding, ruled by the Dege king. In 1727, the Chinese Qing dynasty established a formal protectorate over Kham. Despite claims to Kham territory, the Chinese ambans or political representatives, like governors, rarely went beyond Kangding, leaving areas to the west largely under the control of the King of Chala and other autonomous principalities. The Gyu pass to the west of Kangding was a formidable, physical barrier to the movement of the Chinese army, posing a major obstacle to local administration of Kham by the Chinese.

Western China has seen much change in the last 100 years. At the end of the 19th century, the region of Western Sichuan called Kham, now the Ganze Autonomous Prefecture was, as noted, mostly part of Chala, ruled by the Chala king. In 1903 the Central Tibetan Government attempted to annex the entire territory but the British came to the defense of the Chala King. Later treaties enforced the traditional Tibetan territorial boundary at Chamdo. However, the Chala king lost his authority because of the territorial dispute. The Chinese army headquartered at Chengdu took a renewed interest in the area largely because of the British influence in the region.

Most of Kham had been beyond much direct control by the Chinese until the early 20th century. General Zhao Er-Feng led several military incursions to support new Chinese communities and put down local Khampa opposition to these settlements. His dream of creating a new province was realized several years after his death when the Guomingtang established the new province of Sikang, in 1936. For much of the 20s and 30s, there was much instability in Kham with attacks against non-Gelukpa monasteries by monk-soldier armies from Lhasa, raids by Khampa brigands, taxation by Chinese warlords, and incursions by the Guomingtang military. The Guomingtang created considerable local resentment and hostility by building a road from Chengdu to Tachienlu, another name for Kangding, taxing the locals and forcing many to work on the project. Road building eventually continued to Litang in the west, and north towards Manigango. This social and political instability affected the monasteries, the teaching schedules at the monasteries, and influenced Chinese interest in Tibetan Buddhist theory and practice.

Approximately half the population of Sikang was members of 12 different tribal groups, speaking variants of Qiangic, a language group within Sino-Tibetan, which includes Minyak. Under the Guomingtang these 12 groups, the Zhaba, Queyu, Muya (Minyak), Heishui, Ersu, Baima, Pumi, Jiarong, Ergong, Shixing, Niamuyi, and Guiqiong people had almost complete autonomy. Some of the tribal chieftains had traditionally been approved by the Chinese emperor although the role of tribal chief was usually hereditary. These groups are culturally Tibetan, but influence from the Lhasa government was limited, what little there was coming through monasteries with a connection to the Lhasa government. Many tribes were followers of the pre-Buddhist Bonpo as well as the older Tibetan schools of Buddhism, the Nyingmapa and Kagyupa.

In October of 1934, Mao Tse Tung and the Red Army began the Long March, passing from south to north through the territories of many of these tribal people. The army had to negotiate with tribal chiefs and encountered armed resistance to the incursion on local territory. Later on, after the establishment of the Peoples' Republic of China, what had been Sikang Province under the Guomingtang again became part of Sichuan. Several autonomous prefectures were established for some of the tribal groups.

The dozen years from the late 30s until the founding of the People's Republic of China would be a period of increased propagation of Buddhist teachings, and the continued cooperation between Chinese and Tibetan students in this effort.[229]

Buddhism in Kham

As a hagiography, or spiritual biography, or hagiography, this book is not written in a traditional Tibetan style but does hold somewhat to a traditional Tibetan biography structure in the outline of the important stages in the religious career of a Tibetan lama-monk, detailing the main events of a very busy life. However, setting the biography in the context of the history and culture of the Minyak people, and including sections devoted to descriptions of the activities and administration of Minyak monasteries reflects the greater sensitivity to social and economic life in modern Tibetan writing. The Minyak tribal group has, except for the occasional articles in scholarly journals and several books about the Xixia, who, although they called themselves Minyak[230] are still identified as a separate group, has received scant attention for its role in Central Asian history. Because of the tragic destruction during the Cultural Revolution in China of so much of the

documents, art, and artifacts that might have illuminated the biography, and allowed for it to be presented in a different way, it is written using what the author calls "brief remembrances", personal recollections of the author and others.

Gangkar Rinpoche was a monk belonging to the Kagyu-Nyingma school of Buddhism. This Buddhist sect formed gradually over many centuries, merging the practices and philosophical teachings of several different Buddhist lineages. One of these began in the late 8th century when Padmasambhava was invited to Tibet from India by King Trisong detsen, when he was having problems building a monastery. Padmasambhava, also known as Guru Rinpoche, was originally from an area north of Afghanistan called Orgyan, probably part of Sogdiana.[231] He established the first monastery in Tibet at Samye in 779. The collection of texts and spiritual practices taught by Guru Rinpoche would come to be known by other sects as teachings of the "Ancient Ones" or the Nyingmapa in Tibetan. Several hundred years later another group of teachers would come to Tibet leading a second diffusion of Buddhism. Some Tibetans were able, during this period, to undertake the difficult journey to India to study with Buddhist teachers at Buddhist universities, returning to Tibet as trained practitioners and translators. One was Marpa Lotsawa or Marpa the Translator (1012-1096), a scholar/farmer who supported his travels to India through modest success in gold mining investments. Marpa studied with the highly-accomplished Indian yogi/scholar Naropa. Marpa's most famous student was the poet and yogi Milarepa. The Kagyu school is known for its method of teaching in which a teacher will directly advise the student, in a "spoken (Ka) transmission" (gyu) style of spiritual instruction, hence its name. By the 12 century, the streams of philosophical ideas and spiritual practices in both the Nyingma and Kagyu schools would become unified within the Karma Kagyu, one of four major

Kagyu branches, headed by the Karmapa, whose name was given to the sect.

Another branch of the Nyingma, known today as the Sakyapa, would include practices based on the *Hevajratantra*, translated and taught by Dromi, a contemporary of Marpa. Later, in the late 14th century, Tsongkhapa, hailing from northeast Tibet, would establish the Gelukpa order in reaction to what he perceived as laxity in observance of the Buddhist precepts and vows of conduct by monks and laypeople belonging to the already established sects. The Gelukpa would not only re-affirm ethical conduct and the observance of monastic vows but would be strong supporters of the Dalai Lamas. The Gelukpa were appointed the "official" order when Mongolian armies provided support for the Dalai Lama in the early 1600's during a rebellion against the central Tibetan government.

The four major branches of Tibetan Buddhism each had their particular emphasis or what might be loosely called a "style". To briefly touch on the different Tibetan Buddhist lineages so the non-specialist can have some sense of the "style" of each lineage, one could say the Kagyu were famous as practitioners of meditation, based on its lineage from the cave-dwelling Milarepa who preferred the quiet of the mountains for meditation practice. The contemplative order of the Cistercians or the Benedictines would be a similar group in Christianity. The Sakyapa are famous for clearly-written exposition of Buddhist philosophical views, brilliance in art, and ritual dance. The Nyingma, closely associated with both the Kagyu and Sakya as mentioned (see above), are also recognized for scholarly exposition of the central ideas taught from the time of Padmasambhava, and renowned from the earliest days for their attainments in meditation. They are also known for the controversial practice of discovering texts, called *terma* or hidden treasures, believed to have been hidden by

Padmasambhava or his disciples with the specific intent that the texts would be revealed some time in the future when the teachings in the *terma* would address conditions or issues of the time. The Gelukpa became famous for debate, exposition of the "central view" and analysis of ways of knowing reality as presented in Buddhist philosophy. All four sects supported the practice of meditation, some more than others, and philosophical stances of teachers from different lineages were often the basis for debate about the sorts of experiences possible in meditation. It was common for some sects to emphasize spiritual practice over study and vice versa but the ideal practitioner was one who could intellectually understand the philosophical basis for and fully experience the non-intellectual, intuitive realm of spiritual experience.

However, the teachings of the major Buddhist sects were not the only basis for the world-views of people of Kham. Many tribal groups, though strongly influenced by Tibetan culture, retained early pre-Buddhist beliefs and were followers of local folk-religions. Some regarded forests, springs, whole mountain ranges or specific peaks as sacred. These cultures have been described[232] as animistic or shamanistic.

Gangkar Rinpoche was educated in a system which exposed him primarily to the teachings of the Kagyu, Nyingma, and Sakya schools but included some studies with teachers from the Gelukpa when he traveled to Central Tibet. The Gelukpa did not have as strong a presence as the other sects in the Dege area of Kham where Gangkar Rinpoche received the core of his monastic education. You will also notice that the biography outlines the texts used in a traditional Tibetan monastic education available at Dege in the early 20th century. These educational resources were especially available for an "incarnate lama", one of a line of individuals, each believed to be the reincarnation of his predecessor, in the "born-again" (yang srid) system originating in the Karma Kagyu Buddhist lineage.

The education system at Dege by the time Gangkar Rinpoche went there to study was already in a state of change. By the mid-19th century, the political atmosphere in Tibet was tense with rivalry and disputes between the various regional governing entities. These tensions were intensified by global conflict between Russia and Britain, resulting in the British invasion of Tibet in 1904 to counteract what British intelligence believed to be hostile Russian intrusion in the area. There had been a series of interventions by Western countries in China and after the fall of the Qing dynasty many parts of China were no longer under the direct control of the central government but governed by local warlords, some even supported, before and during WWII, by foreign intelligence groups.[233] Because of the links between patronage of monasteries and local government or warlord rule, Buddhist monasteries were affected by the tensions between the central Tibetan government at Lhasa and non-Tibetan principalities in the eastern part of the Tibetan plateau. These tensions were already present before international tensions would influence Tibetan affairs even more. That political disputes became entwined with sectarian philosophical disagreements compounded the instability in business and life in general for those on the Tibetan plateau.

Three leading Khampa scholar-monks, Jamgon Kongtrul (1813-1890), Jamyang Khyentse (1820-1892), and Chogyur Lingpa (1829-1870) could see greater disruption to the social order if disputes continued with no change in the attitudes of the followers of the different schools. The three men: a Kagyu/Nyingmapa, a follower of the Sakyapa, and a Nyingmapa respectively, individually collected ancient texts. Their work of discovering, editing, reprinting, and collating Tibetan texts was proceeded by the work of Jigme Lingpa (1730-98) who also compiled many older texts from different traditions. His cycle of teachings called the Longchen Nyingtig provided much of the later emphasis on yogic practice and direct experience of Buddhist teachings. All were leaders in the creation of a non-sectarian (*ris-med*, pronounced 'ree may') movement, based on an emphasis of the common features and ideas shared by the various Buddhist sects. Kongtrul, Khyentse, and Chogyur Lingpa encouraged debate and dialogue. The stress was on tolerance and a willingness to work with other groups. This tolerance was an essential part of the ris-med movement and came from its emphasis on direct experience and the idea that awakening was a pure openness not limited by conventional logic and arbitrary distinctions. The non-sectarian approach was also a reflection of the desire to protect lesser-known lineages of spiritual practice, as seen in the compilation of texts, and as defense against the standardization of practice and debate as emphasized by the Gelukpa. At the core of much of the debate was the long-standing contrast between very different views or interpretations of the central concept of "*sunyata.*"

Gangkar Rinpoche received his training within this new non-sectarian educational style as it was evolving in the early 20th century. An example of the non-sectarian emphasis of the *ri-med* movement could be found in a monastic curriculum where philosophical points-of-view might be debated according to the perspectives of different schools rather than just one; physical training techniques meant to help those sitting in meditation for long periods keep healthy would be adopted from various methods; and different approaches to meditation practices would be taught according to the special practices unique to each sect or uniquely suited to the background of the student. Contributing to this flexibility in teaching was the ecumenical style in Kongtrul's collecting, cataloguing and editing five large collections of texts, teachings from the major Tibetan Buddhist lineages, achieving an early archiving of Tibetan Buddhist spiritual culture. A student might study the "path and fruit" teachings of the Sakyapa, use spiritual practices derived from the Kagyupa or the "view" according to the Nyingmapa, and learn logical debate and analysis according to Gelukpa methods. Openness to the teachings of different sects did not mean that a student would get an education that was only a hodge-podge of ideas from several different schools. A student of the Kagyu would focus on study of Kagyu texts and engage in practices emphasized by the Kagyu. The ecumenical approach was exemplified in the teaching curriculum at Dege monasteries in the late 19th century and onwards until the late 1940s. Nowadays, the legacy of this approach can be seen in current textbooks used in the universities for minorities in which core ideas of each sect are presented as separate chapters in one book.

The emphasis on openness in teaching would be later shown in Gangkar Rinpoche becoming one of the first lamas to teach students from other cultures. His openness to ideas inspired students who would influence the formal adoption of teaching Tibetan culture and Buddhist philosophy in schools and universities in China, the development of Tibetan studies and the establishment of schools in China for ethnic minorities.

Chogyam Trungpa[234] was one of the early Khampa lamas to write of his education in a monastery devoted to the *ri-me* movement, and of his studies with teachers who were the disciples of Kongtrul, Khyentse, and Chogyur Lingpa. Grey Tuttle has written the first account of the role of Tibetan teachers in China during the period before the formation of the People's Republic of China.

Despite the slow implementation of the ris-med movement's approach to education in the monasteries, many parts of the traditional monastic education were made available to lay people as well as monks through the creation of new schools in Minyak and elsewhere in Kham. However, political and economic tensions would be seen in local disputes and conflict in many parts of Kham. These events, long before those following the establishment of the People's Republic of China in 1949, have been described by Jackson, who writes of Khenpo Gangshar's attempts at opening up the monasteries to allow laypeople to attend teachings and Teachman , who observed the conditions in Chala and Dege firsthand(see Bibliography).

Appendix B

Minyak according to Tibetan history and an analysis of some Minyak naming conventions[235]

By Minyak Gonpo

Minyak comprised lGa, lDong and rMu which came from six lineages of the Mi'u people who were Tibetan ancestors. In the east were the rGya nag [Chinese], the 'Jang in the south, the sTod bod [Tibetans] in the west, and Sogs po [Mongolians] in the North. In the middle of this region was Minyak known as lower mDo consisting of Gha and other places [Amdo area] and the area known as Greater Minyak consisting of upper mDo and Kham Minyak.

When Tibet was no longer expanding, Minyak had reached a time of unequaled influence. This power remained through 4 rulers in the Sung Dynasty starting in the first calendrical cycle in the Water Monkey year (1032) and lasting until the fourth calendrical cycle in the Fire Pig year (1227). From the rule of the Minyak King Si-hu there were 9 dynasties to the last King rGod rDo-rje dPal. rDo-rje dPal is known in Mongolian as Shri-tur Go-thul Ken-han-kan. The Chinese, using the word 'hu' in 'Si hu', called him Ruler Hu (Hu-wang).

During the sixth Minyak ruling period, the capital moved to Gharu. An agent of the ruler sought to expand the kingdom and went to upper mNga' ris [Western Tibet]. Based on his control of the sTag region and the Seng Ge valley, he became an administrator serving the Sa-skya ruler. The lineage of the gTsang-pa Sa-skya ruler rGyal-rtse Chos-rgyal also comes from the line of the Shar-kha-ba who moved to gTsang from Minyak. 'Brug [Bhutan] and 'Bras-ljongs [Sikkim] royal families are descendents of the Minyak king.

When Buddhist teachings were on the decline in upper and middle gTsang, there was a great decline in knowledge. However, there were many Minyak Phan-khon monasteries, and the study and explication of the arts and sciences was wide spread. Before Atisa went to Tibet (in 1042) he lived as a scholar at Nalendra in India. The Tsa-mi translator, who died in India, Sang-rgyas grags, was there as was Rong seng-ge grags, the teacher of bLa- chen dgongs-pa rab-gsal (952-1035). First there was Kva-'od mchog-grags, the translator from what is nowadays lJang, and the great Shar-pa-ba.

Later, many scholars would come such as the Five Minyak Wise Ones. Tibetan arts and sciences became widely established in an environment free of competing influences. The nephew and uncle of Sa Pan and the translators of the Yuan king were Minyak people. For that reason Minyak history is an important part of Tibetan history.

Among Tibetan historical books there are genealogies, annals, histories, archives of clans, and monastic lines. Out of these many categories there is the Minyak cycle. There is the so-called Minyak royal genealogy and Minyak spiritual histories found in dPa'-bo Rin-po-che's "Festival of the Wise Ones". Although there is some explanation on how sacred teachings (of the Buddha) spread to Minyak, here is nothing said regarding the total picture of this process or how Minyak is an important part in Tibetan histories. Even what we call the Minyak royal genealogies are nothing but a repetition of the stories of the history of the lineage by Minyak Tsen tse Shes rab ye shes, such as "A God's Story".

Here, so that we can scientifically examine the real history of Minyak, first we can examine some of the names of the Minyak kings. Minyak King Sihu gets his name from the Minyak language 'Si' meaning "day" and 'hu' meaning "night" thus indicating a king who rules "day and night." This is similar to the eulogy "Long Life" used by the Chinese. 'Gri rgyu' is also found in Tibetan and Chinese documents from Sichuan, and 'Si'u,' a variant of Si-hu.

The Minyak King Tsami takes his name from the Minyak words 'tsa' meaning 'earth' and 'mi' (meaning) 'heaven'. The "King of Heaven and Earth" or the "Lord of Heaven and Earth" are expressions used in praise of the king's power. We find written in some old Tibetan texts **ra** super scribed over **tsa** and so people say "rtsa mi shing" (straw or wooden man). These are just stories with no connection to historical reality.

After the Minyak people seized the previous capital, he was called King Minyak Tang-kus. In the Minyak language, even now, silk cloth is called Tang-skus. Since China is the source of this natural resource, when he became a king in China he was called the "Silk King." This is the meaning behind this name. In earlier Tibetan texts we find "Tang khun" and "Tong kun." Even in some old texts we find rGya tong-khun[236] rgyal-po (the "Chinese Silk King"). All of these expressions are corruptions of the word Tang-kus. It is clear that even the Chinese word "Tangxiang" comes from name Tang-kus.

The last capital of the Minyak kings was lGa-chu-sngon-mdo. Chu is "su cu" in the Minyak language. The place (mdo) where the rivers (chu) converge ('dus) is called Cu-sngon-mdo. There are many such places in Khams Minyak. The lGa, area (getting its name) from the great Tibetan lGa clan, was controlled by Minyak for a long time. In Tibetan, although there is a group of words such as lga, gha, sga, all have one meaning [ginger]. Cu-sngon-mdo has changed its spelling in Tibetan texts (the word written as) sKye-dgu-mdo and sKye-rgu-mdo with only slight changes in pronunciation.

122

The capital for the Minyak king of upper mDo Khams was Dar-rtsi-mdo. In the Minyak language 'dar' is "silk" and 'rtsi' has the meaning of "medicine." This is the place where there was an exchange of silk and medicines between the Tibetans and Han; it is famous by that name. In old Chinese texts the pronunciation is transliterated as Ta can lu'u (Tatsenlu).

After the capital of Minyak was seized by the Mongolians, the king was called "chief" (dpon) as ruler of Minyak. After the deterioration of the Mongolian (state) the ruler of Kham Minyak had the title lCags la rgyal po (the King at Iron (Mountain). The Ming (Ta min) emperor gave him the title "Chief of Ming Zheng" (Min Kring thu'u si), with the lineage continuing up to now. The palace "Rig gnas gsar brje" (Changing to New Learning") is gone without a trace. Ruins are all that is left of Iron Mountain. After northern Minyak was conquered by the Mongolians, some descendents of King Si hu escaped to Kham Minyak and settled there. On the bSam dbang plain one can still see the ruins of King Si hu's palace. The valley below there is called Si'u rong these days. The jurisdiction of Khams Minyak included all of rTa'u rdzong, the lower part of Brag 'go rdzong, upper part of Dam-pa rdzong, the lower parts of Nyag-rong and nyag-chu- rdzong, all of Dar-mdo rdzong, part of the rMi-li autonomous region, rBu-rong rdzong Pal-mo-che, and the upper part of Sag-rnga-khongs Hri-mi'an rdzong. There were many peoples, towns and monasteries. Yet in the 16th era and during the 10th Tibetan calendrical cycle these were attacked many times by the evil Mongolian troops of Gu shri shog. All the monasteries and encampments were broken up and ordinary towns, houses, grazing lands, crop lands, and wilderness: all wiped clean of any culture. It became a gloomy place. As no more than a few of the Mi nyag people escaped the killing, even the language, in a day, was diminished and scattered across China.

When we examine the history of the previous thousand years, over many centuries, it is very important to pay attention to names of people and places. For example in the name of a hill in lGa, found in the Beijing People's Publishing House edition of the Red Annals, at the end of a series of terms in chapter 27 are 'Si no'i zhva'. As the twelfth in a series in chapter 28 there is "Si no'i nag" and associated with it are 'Si no'i shan' and 'He'i no'i hran.' All these different syllables occur in one book. In the Sichuan Peoples Publishing House edition of the "Chinese-Tibetan Nest of Letters" they have 'Si no'i wa'. If we look at look at the original words written as footnotes by the writer of the Red Annals and we look at the name of the mountain we have "Zhva nag shag hran", clearly a Chinese word. If we talk of a mountain and say that it is dark, we say it is "nying." But if one were to speak of a "Black Heart (Hill)", in the Minyak language we say "'bo sems nying" or "sems nag." From these we get "Si no'i shan" or "Si no'i wa" with no need to go on here. If we look at the back and forth exchange of ideas over time, there are errors at the time of publication. First it has not been possible from the beginning to organize the sounds of the Minyak dialect. As to syllables found in histories, if one looks at a few of the Minyak terms in word lists it is not possible to see these are Chinese words. When translating the language of another people, since the Minyak dialect is based on many different styles of writing from the south and west and all kinds of problems are encountered, this is something for the long term. Therefore we can take a look at each one of the words now on hand, trusting in the explanation of the terms and research those. Since there is the danger of there being no results for our efforts if we go off too far on tangents, for truer meaning of history we will be able to research thoroughly the real Minyak language. If we understand the true history of Minyak, it is certain that we will open up a wider perspective.

Appendix C

A Visit to Minyak

Following a Pilgrim's Trail on the Western Slopes of Gongga Shan (2003)

The following is an account of 10 days[237] travel in September, 2003 to a small part of Kham traditionally called Minyak or Kham-Minyak. The purpose of this journey was to visit monasteries, shrines, homes, and sacred sites mentioned in the biography of Gangkar Rinpoche, the previous abbot of several monasteries in Minyak. These monasteries are famous in Kham history of the last 100 years and are where many in the core group of Tibet specialists in

China studied. We visited a tiny, but historically very important, corner of Minyak. I have added some background on how I became involved in the study of Minyak and its role in Kham history. All other views and comments related to the 2003 journey are solely those of the translator.

Introduction

It was not my intention to specifically study Kham history but was drawn to the subject while in Kham looking for Tibetan texts from the Kagyu[238] sect of Tibetan Buddhism. During a visit in 1999, I was invited into a private home near sDe-dge and given access to the family collection of Tibetan texts. The name of a region of Kham called Minyak kept showing up in some of the books I looked through. After I found the name mentioned a half-dozen times in the week I spent in the private archives, my curiosity grew. The only information about Minyak found at the time was that it was a location of monasteries for the Kagyu and Sakya sects. Minyak was described in glowing terms as "the best", "sublime," a place where monks would go for advanced study or for spiritual retreat, sparking my curiosity even more. Several informants mentioned that people in Minyak spoke a language that was hard to understand.

I later read modern Tibetan histories and research articles in libraries in Beijing. I learned that Minyak has been an important part of Tibetan history. The territory of Minyak used to cover large parts of present-day Qinghai, Ningxia, Gansu, and Sichuan. For the purposes of this account, I will focus on the Kham (Sichuan) part of Minyak. The Minyak people were called the Xi Xia during the Sung Dynasty (960-1279). The Xi Xia (1027-1227) are also known as the Tanguts by Western historians, taking the Minyak word for "silk cloth", a title given to the Minyak ruler at the height of the Minyak kingdom's influence, in reference to tributes of silk cloth made to the Minyak or Xixia ruler. In 1227, Genghis Khan and his armies destroyed the capital of the Xixia or Tangut kingdom. Heirs to the throne escaped and gradually moved to the south to establish their capital at present-day Kangding (*Dar-brtse-mdo*). The palace was "at Iron Mountain" or Charila (*lcags-ri-la*) in Tibetan, shortened to Chala (*lCags-la*) The name is still seen on street and building signs in Kangding as Iron Mountain (lcags-ri on Tibetan signs). Minyak is thus another name for the kingdom of Chala, ruled by the King at Iron Mountain for several hundred years until 1904.

The central Tibetan government attempted to take over the territory of Chala in 1903 but the British came to the aid of the Chala king.[239] The Tibetans were stopped at Chamdo. The lines bounding the Tibetan territory were reconfirmed and agreed to by the Tibetans at the time. Today they form the eastern border of the Tibetan Autonomous Region (TAR).[240] The Chala king had revealed the limits of his power and lost much of his political influence after the 1904 incident. The Chinese government, the Guomingtang, took advantage of the power vacuum and showed a renewed interest in Chala. The entire Chala-Kham-Minyak region was incorporated into a new province called Sikang in 1930. After the revolution in 1949, Sikang was dissolved. The Ganze Autonomous Prefecture now covers most of what comprised Sikang. A significant portion of Minyak is also included in the Kangding Autonomous Prefecture which shares with the Ganze Autonomous Prefecture (GAP) responsibility for highway maintenance and other administrative projects such as the census. There is some overlap in responsibilities for education and public health as well. Many buildings in Minyak are marked with placards indicating the building as under the registry of the Kangding Autonomous Prefecture.

For the Karma Kargyu sect of Tibetan Buddhism, Minyak has been a center of learning during the last 100 years. A primary source of information about Minyak has been The Incarnation from White Glacier Mountain, the biography of Gangkar Rinpoche, Chokyi Senge, by Minyak Gongbu, the foremost Minyak scholar alive today. I decided to translate the biography and worked on the translation with Gongbu in Beijing during the autumn of 2001. Two Kagyu monasteries on my list of sites to see in Minyak, Kham-sum-drak (pronounced Ku-see drak) monastery and its retreat or practice monastery, Gangkar, were well-known centers of learning, open to students of Gangkar Rinpoche from all parts of China. One student at both monasteries, Garma C.C. Chang, is familiar to American students of Buddhism as the translator of the Hundred Thousand Songs of Milarepa. Several students continued academic work on the history of Buddhism in China and helped form what is the formal study of Tibet in China, Tibetology (*Xi-zang wen-xue*).

In the back of the biography is a brief guide by Gangkar Rinpoche to sacred sites near Minyak monasteries. I knew it would be a challenge working with the guidebook, what people in Kham call a "*lam-yig*", written more than eighty years ago. As Gangkar Rinpoche noted, the guide was a compilation of material from earlier sources, not mentioned by name; some are local tradition, others described as "hidden texts" (terma, mentioned above). The guidebook was written for Buddhist pilgrims and therefore it was assumed that readers would be entirely familiar with discussion of meditation and sacred sites. In Tibetan Buddhist practice places considered sacred are often given this description because of experiences during the prolonged practice of meditation. Visions and dreams that result from such practice come to be associated with the places in which they occur. The miraculous appearance of springs, foot prints left on rock, and other "wondrous" events also contribute to the aura of the sacred, what some poets have called the mysterious presence at sacred sites.

128

A statement in the guidebook, repeated in other texts I had seen, attributed to the 3rd Karmapa, Rangjung Dorje, that Minyak was the best place for meditation in Kham was the main inspiration for travel to Minyak from the start, to see the place for myself, and try to understand what the Karmapa may have meant by his statements about the quality of meditation in the environment of Minyak. Meditation practice has been a daily activity of mine for years. I start each day with what the Chinese call *da-zuo*, "just sitting." Since my first trip to China, I have traveled to China with the intent to visit at least one sacred Buddhist or Daoist site and to seek spiritual renewal and inspiration at caves, shrines, or monasteries where Buddhist sages lived and practiced meditation. While descriptions in the guidebook of images, footprints on rock, and the benefits gained from visiting certain places in the mountains of Minyak were all good, what would I actually find in Minyak or at Bo Gangkar monastery, the last of the monasteries on my list to visit?

A major problem would be the condition of trails. Guide books written for sites at mountains of lower elevation, with many more visitors on pilgrimage, may see fewer changes in trails over time because of better trail maintenance or weather patterns. Gangkar monastery is located on a ridge above Gangkar Shan glaciers. Rock fall, glacier melt, earth movements from earthquakes and rain are a constant source of change, a challenge to anyone seeking clearly-defined routes even if trails were maintained. Then there was the pointless destruction wrought by the so-called Cultural Revolution. Both Kham-sum-drak and Gangkar monasteries were destroyed and are now mostly rebuilt with refurnishing of temple statues, paintings, and banners in the finishing stages. Traditionally people would study at Kham-sum-drak and then go to Gangkar monastery to practice meditation either at the monastery or at retreat huts or caves in the vicinity.

Impermanence, the inevitability of change, is one of the central maxims of Buddhist thought. Accomplished meditators, older members of the *sangha* or spiritual community, monks who spent most of their time at an older monastery would talk about the destruction of a monastery as sad, but as an event that was over, in the past, not something that hadn't happened before. The history of monastery buildings in Minyak is one of destruction, decay, collapse, with monasteries and temples sometimes rebuilt, sometimes not. This has been the case since the invasion of Genghis Khan's armies in the 11th century. Monasteries have even changed sect affiliation. For example, many monasteries historically under the administration of parent Kagyu monasteries are now associated with the Gelukpa sect.

Once you leave Kangding traveling West and cross the "Gyu pass" (Tibetan: *rgyud-la*), which has somehow become transformed in popular guidebooks to the "Gyemi pass", one enters into Minyak territory. The primary language spoken there is Minyak or Muya, which is not a dialect of Chinese or Tibetan. You come to a major fork in the road at Dzongzhab. The main route south of Dzongzhab towards Jiarong in the Yi Autonomous Prefecture is marked with signs indicating the distance from the main junction at Dzongzhab. The Minyak indicate every place as "along the river" (*sa-sde-chus*), followed by the kilometer indicator. For example, a village may be "on the river at (kilometer) 75." The exception to the use of a general descriptor is the name of the main village, or main transportation hub, pronounced "Saw-day-chews" or "Saw day"[241] which might be rendered as "nice river place." The name once given to the village to indicate its pleasing qualities is in marked contrast to the pungent smells and gross images that assault one's senses these days. The town is noisy, a meeting place for every passer by, with many motorcycles and even a motorcycle dealership.

We went north on the Tung Chu, a tributary of the Yalong, to spend the day hiking into the back country at a "place along the river at 52." We hiked a trail for several miles before coming to a canyon that led up to the birthplace of the previous Gangkar Rinpoche. The local people were busy harvesting barley and giant radishes. Many gladly joined our group to show us impressions of hand and footprints left in rocks by Gangkar Rinpoche when he was a child.

The next day, at "on the river, point 75", we stopped at a small village with steep mountain cliffs towering above it. Canyons held remaining patches of old-growth forest. The rest had been clear-cut in the 50s but now hill sides are lush with 40-50 year old second growth. We left motor transportation behind at Kham-sum-drag monastery, perched on a hillside at 12,300 feet.

This newly-rebuilt Kargyu monastery was famous for much of the 20th century as one of the most important learning centers in Kham. It was the first monastery open to non-Tibetan students, because of the non-sectarian, ecumenical policies of its director, Gangkar Rinpoche. We were also on the 5th day of ascent in the mountains. The village "on the river, point 52" is about 11,500 feet altitude. We had been steadily ascending to about 12,300 feet, a level we would remain at, on the average, for the next week, crossing the Tsemi Pass (roughly 15,700) and to trek on a ridge above the Gongga Shan glacier to about 17,800 feet altitude. It takes about a week to feel entirely normal at high altitude. Though we would be at a not-very-high altitude by mountaineering standards and for only ten days, every day was spent doing a lot of hiking, walking back into many canyons to visit sacred sites.

At the main gate, the entrance to Kham-sum-drak monastery is a 6' by 6' flow chart publicly documenting the participation of local people in the rebuilding of the monastery. The chart listed the name of the local village, and a list of villagers' names, showing either the number of volunteer hours a villager put in working in reconstruction tasks or the amount of a cash donation.

Since the Chinese revolution, the means of support for monastic communities has completely changed. Support for monasteries used to come from their large land holdings, with much of the property leased to farmers. Part of each year's crop was owed to the land-owning monastery. Loans made to the farmer were with interest, often at rates of 100% or higher in some parts of Tibet. Debt of some farming families spanned generations. In addition was the frequent expectation that male children would be given over to the monastery. Perhaps the most onerous practice was the system of corvée, or provision of uncompensated transportation services on demand. Imagine starting to eat dinner when there is a knock on the door, and a government official demands that you go out and rent a U-Haul truck, drive from New York, where you live, to Chicago, pick up a load of goods, and drive back to New York with the load. You pay for the rental, gas, time off work. That would be corvée. Land ownership and corvée ended with the revolution. Without the money from land leasing, interest from loans, and free transportation services, monasteries became hard-pressed for financial support. After most of the monasteries in Kham were destroyed during the Cultural Revolution, support for remaining monasteries was minimal. Since county governments are now financially responsible for the rebuilding of temples, pavilions, monasteries and small shrines, and the county (or the autonomous prefecture) governments are also hard-pressed for cash, how do the monasteries get rebuilt? For places like Kham-sum-drak, former students at the original monastery have established "dharma-centers" or small monasteries at places outside China, such as Taiwan. These "children" of the "parent" monastery are providing the tens of thousands of US dollars used in rebuilding the monastery.

The CEO of a group of monasteries is often the head of the main monastery for the sect. For the Karma Kagyu (*Karma bKa-brgyud-pa*), monastic administration in Kham is technically carried out from Palpung (*dPal-spungs*), at De-ge (*sDe-dge*), under the direction of the Tai Situ Rinpoche, who is now based in India. These administrative units have also raised substantial amounts for the reconstruction effort. Building materials are provided locally and traditional suppliers of high-quality Buddha-statues in Amdo (northeast Tibet) now provide the Buddhist instruments and supports for the faithful.

After several days at the Kham-sum-drak monastery, horses were hired for the long trek (10+ hours) from the mother monastery to Gangkar, the retreat monastery on a ledge above the Gongga Shan glacier on the western side of Gongga Shan, reputed to be a very supportive environment for meditation. The next day we mounted horses led by two Minyak men, one a monk from the monastery, our destination. One of the first things I said to the horsemen in my rusty Kham dialect was to offer an apology for all of us novice riders in not knowing how to ride well, unlike people of Kham who are such good riders. At first we had a hard time mounting and dismounting, our riding muscles not fully stretched until the next day. At 93kg, my weight was too much for Tibetan horses used to carrying less. I noticed my horse was having a hard time when we started up the Tsemi Pass.

We had a most pleasant ride up the Yulungxi River valley, visiting several old sites, perhaps the most important a building constructed by the famous bridge-builder, architect, poet and musician, Thangtong Gyalpo (1361-1485), whose parents were Minyakpa. We passed through five villages before reaching the turnoff for the Tsemi Pass.

At the Tsemi Pass the horse I was riding made a stretching movement while going up a steep slope. The

133

stretching movement loosened the saddle. It came undone and I was sent crashing down off the right side. I checked to see if cameras were not damaged. I was a bit shaken so decided to walk the rest of the way up the pass. Another member of our group was later unceremoniously dropped on the ground by the same horse.

From the top of the pass to the small Minyakpa village of Tsemi, travelers are advised to walk down the path until it gets less steep. We were all glad to do so. The trail was narrow, the drop-offs hundreds of feet. Many loads of goods, including mountaineering equipment belonging to groups heading to climb Gongga Shan have been lost or damaged on the Tsemi pass.

In Tsemi we met the village elder, an amiable, erudite scholar to whom we gave some Kagyu yoga books. The ride up to the monastery from Tsemi follows a steep trail down and across a log bridge, then up a series of switchbacks to a wider, more gradual path. This trail continues up the ridge through a forest draped in moss.

Huge wild boar with frighteningly-long tusks crashed through the trees, running quite fast. A mysterious white horse, almost aglow in its vitality, larger than other local horses, appeared mysteriously out of fog and mist. I thought about the horse later that evening and wondered whether it had been a "spirit horse." Then the monastery itself appeared, enveloped in fog swirling up from the valley below.

Gangkar monastery with sacred rock in foreground

We visited with the few residents, found candles, and arranged our gear in the room we were given up in the back of the monastery on the second floor. Eventually we got some hot water and had some noodles before turning in for the night.

The next morning after a breakfast of butter tea and *tsampa*, or barley flour, one of the monks took us out to view sacred objects, all stones: boulders with hand or foot prints, marks left by yaks on rock, scratches on stones from ritual objects used during subjugation of evil spirits. The meadows and forest around the monastery have lots of these sorts of phenomena associated with unusual events in the lives of Buddhist adepts who once lived in the area. Marks on rocks are mentioned in the "Guide Book" I was in the end able to visit and document a good portion of the sites mentioned in the "Guide Book." I was not able to make it to some sites because trails were gone or inaccessible. I had to remind myself from time to time, to dampen my innate enthusiasm to try to see absolutely everything I was already seeing many more undocumented sites than I expected.

Dorje Lodro (*rDo-rje blo-gros*), spirit protector of
Gonga Shan

I grabbed film and cameras and started hiking up the
ridge above the monastery. I remembered reading an article
in one of the **Mountaineers** publications that mentioned a
ridge from which Joseph Rock had taken some photographs
of the Gonga Shan glacier in 1929 while on an expedition
sponsored by the National Geographic Society. Great views

of the Gonga Shan glacier could be found from this ridge if one took a trail that started from the spring at Gangkar monastery. The trail ascends through a forest, and just above tree level, at around 13,800 feet, there are ruins of a retreat hut. When I reached tree-line, all the clouds and fog lifted from Gongga Shan. I was overjoyed to see the peak in all its glory. I continued up the ridge through meadows of yellow flowers and purple iris. The higher I went, the better the views of the glacier. I could see how glacier collapse, shrinkage, falling boulders and changes in stream flows had altered the terrain. One of the trails I had asked about was no longer accessible because of this. Still, key markers mentioned in the pilgrims' guide, three lakes with small islands, were clearly visible; as well a good portion of what is described in the guide as the "middle part of the mountain."

View of Gongga Shan from the hermitage

Coming back down the ridge, I took a detour to the ruins of an old hermitage. I had decided when it would be an excellent spot for a long meditation. I had already sat in the Guru Rinpoche temple in the monastery the previous afternoon. The energy in that place had been riveting and only because I began to feel the inside dampness from the light frost forming on the outside of my fleece jacket was I compelled to leave my seat and seek some butter tea.

Now I was able to sit in this old hermitage. A deep calm filled my body and mind. With squirrels scurrying around me and the sounds of birds cooing in the shrubbery, the warmth of the afternoon deepened the calm, clear state of attention. Time seem to stand still for several hours.

I felt the Karmapa was indeed right: Gangkar monastery is one of the best places in Kham for meditation. Gangkar is remote. The environment is delightfully restful, with fresh water, sacred stones and carvings everywhere to remind one of the fine qualities of the place. It is impossible to ignore these markers, the heritage left by the sages who lived and practiced here.

Footnotes to the translation

Comments made by Minyag Gonpo are indicated by MG in parentheses.

[1] intentionality (dgongs)

[2] or "spoon"

[3] Chos-kyi rgya-mtsho, a member of the Gelukpa school, whose monastery was at Ra-na-kha. He was a very good student of Gangkar Rinpoche who studied the Naro chos drug. There were many ring-sril (relics) at his death and rainbows. He told Minyak Gonpo that only he (Gonpo) could write the biography of Gangkar Rinpoche (personal communication from author).

[4] use of the double-negative: lit: "how can one not say that I won't achieve a goal such as this?"

[5] The historical Buddha Sakyamuni.

[6] rgyan drug: p.545 Nagajuna, Aryadeva ('Phags-pa'i lha), Asanga (Thogs-med), Vasubandhu (dByig-gnyen), Phyogs-glang, Chos-grags

[7] mchog gnyis, i.e. Thogs-med (Asanga), kLu-sgrub (Nagajuna)

[8] literally "a wolf honoring one's parents with a sheep's kindness"

[9] gla-rtsi-babs gsum

[10] sum-chu rtsa gsum gyi longs spyod, "like the offerings in a mandala" (MG)

[11] lit: (ches phul du byung) 'one that arises as special'

[12] Queen's Silver

[13] The latest altitude listed in the Japanese Alpine News, Vol. 1, October 2001 is 7556 meters.

[14] see p. 30; p. 501, Tibet Handbook.

[15] Sbyor drug; P. 2029: Bod-rgya tshig mdzod chen mo: 1) so sdud; 2) bsam gtan; 3) srog rtsol; 4) 'dzin-pa; 5) rjes-dran; 6) ting-'dzin-te (Dus 'khor rdzogs rim rlung sbyor): categories of development-phase stabilization of vital energy in the Kalacakra tradition

[16] Bod gna'

[17] knowledge of it, spreading everywhere, like the wind (MG)

[18] The last of a series of temples built by Srong btsan sgam-po.

[19] Yi su zi zhi zhou, Shimian xian, nowadays Yi, not Tibetan

[20] Honorific title "rJe thams-cad mkhyen-pa 'gran-pa'i zla thams-cad dang bral-ba"

[21] phyi-nang; lit. outside/inside

[22] Ma-pham-gi mtsho

[23] sgron shing - pinus tabulai formis

[24] ixeris, "Khrungs-dpe dri-med shel-gyi me-long, p. 264

[25] 'ug-chos me-tog, Incarvillea compacta Maxim

[26] lit: "grass in summer, worm in winter"

[27] saussurea lappa

[28] Mi'u drug: sBa, lDong, 'Bru, sGa, rGo, dPa-yi-tshan, Zla-yi-tshan

[29] "as to the events relevant to when he took power as emperor"

[30] p. 2060, Bod-rgya tshig mdzod chen-mo, under Minyak siu rgyal-po: "In the Earth-Rabbit year of the 1st calendrical cycle (1027), a small group of people called the Thang zhang chang established a capital called Xi-xia at what is nowadays called Ningxia. In the Fire-Pig year of the 4th calendrical cycle it came under the control of the Mongolian Qing-gis (Khan). The royal lineage went to the south. In the six mountain ranges in Kham, Minyak was established to the west of Dartsendo. The tones of the Chinese Shis-zha are changed in Tibetan to Si-hu or Si'u."

[31] Mongolian name (sog skad-MG)

[32] lit: had sexual intercourse with her as the king

[33] The Mongolians say that the Minyag tried to kill the King, and then the Queen drowned in a river. (MG) In a review of the Chinese film, "Xixia Lu Tiaotiao", the director Lu Wei is quoted as saying: "In the 8th century, the nomadic Dangxiang [Minyag] tribe left the highlands of Tibet...and settled in the Hetao region to found the Xixia empire. The

Dangxiang people were so audacious that they believed they had killed the famous Genghis Khan." This view reflects the on-going controversy surrounding this period in China's history.

[34] in Qinghai

[35] the region of sTag, the Seng ge lung, near gShi rga brtse

[36] 'Untamed or wild ruler'

[37] hence silk king (Tangkus) and we get "Tangut" in Western sources.

[38] Speaking Tibetan only nowadays

[39] "King at Iron (Hill)"

[40] The ruins of Iron Hill palace are now enclosed by a wall.

[41] See Schwieger, Peter. "First Steps Towards a History of Don-yod, King of Be-ri, Beijing: Seminar on Tibetan Studies, 1997.

[42] one of the six districts of Kham

[43] Srong-btsan sgam-po's fourth wife was a Minyak woman named Minyak ru-yong bza' rgyal-mo btsun, p. 1294, Gangs-can mkhas-grub rim-byon ming-mdzod

[44] p.555-6, Bod-rgya tshig-mdzod chen-mo

[45] lit. sensitive to what one should accept or reject

[46] These are earth, with adequate sunlight (sa), water (chu), stones, or building material (rdo), trees (shing), decent weather (nam-shis), and five basic Buddhist practices (sangs-rgyas chos lnga).(MG)

[47] Tibetans count the age of a new-born child as one since nine months of gestation are counted (or ten months from conception). Here Gangkar Rinpoche is counted as five in the Tibetan tradition or four in the Western calendar.

[48] The Tibetan term for confidence is *dad-pa*. This word is often translated by the word "faith." The use of faith means something quite different in a Christian context. Tibetans assume experience exists when using the word *dad-pa* (pronounced day-pa) unlike using the word to represent having "faith" in something which one has not experienced. For example, in spoken Tibetan one might say: "Nga la ja dad-pa yod.", "I like tea." It is assumed that you drink tea or

have drunk tea. In Buddhism, confidence is nourished by the experiences one has in spiritual practice. Thus, the more one practices, the more confidence one has.

[49] smon lam rnam lnga (MG)

[50] This monastery no longer exists. (MG)

[51] Both new Gelukpa monasteries with many monks.

[52] Sakyapa monastery, new, originally built by Thang-stong rgyal-po (MG).

[53] Construction at sDe-dge dpal-spungs was started in the Fire-Sheep year of the 12 cycle (1727).

[54] bzo-ba'i rig pa - techniques on building stupas, monasteries; including calligraphy

[55] language (mngon brjod) and rhetoric (sdeb sbyor)

[56] Mkhas-grub gnyis-ldan: 'having the two (qualities) of being both a scholar and realized'. This is another way of saying that one can be well-trained in theory and has put what one knows into practice and so "knows" what one is talking about. This dual quality of personality, to be well-trained in theory and practical application of the theory or ideas, was a trait expected of scholars trained at dPal-spungs. There was recognition of the problem of those who were "all theory and little practice" (rtogs-ge-pa) as well as those practitioners who claimed experience and yet could not intelligently articulate it (rang-bzo'i rnal-'byor-pa).

[57] The mantra Om mani paymay hung.

[58] 'dul gzhung gsan pa'i dbu btsugs

[59] 'Phags-pa yon-tan 'od-kyi gsung 'dul-ba mdo

[60] So-sor thar-pa'i mdo (Pratimoksa Sutra)

[61] mNgon-pa mdzod

[62] mNgon-pa kun-btus

[63] rTsa-ba shes- rab

[64] dBu-ma-la-'jug-pa

[65] dBu-ma bzhi- rgya-pa

[66] Byang-chub-sems-pa'i spyod-pa-la-'jug-pa

[67] Sher-phyin mngon-par rtogs-pa'i rgyan

[68] mDo-sde rgyan

[69] dBu mtha' rnam-'byed

[70] Chos-nyid rnam-'byed

[71] rgyud bla-ma

[72] 'Og-min-du rJe-btsun byams-pa-la mngon-sum zhus-par grags-pa'i spyod-pa

[73] Image of Sakyamuni at Ramoche

[74] rlung, "that which causes movement", motility, the vital energy

[75] Lineage from Taranatha, now in Aba.

[76] By 'Jigs-med gling-pa

[77] theg-dgu'i yang-rtse 'od-gsal:

[78] thugs gtigs chen po

[79] Khyad-par 'phags bstod kyi 'grel pa. Dil-mgo-mkhyen-brtse had a copy of this book and took it with him to India (MG).

[80] Dri lan mkhas pa'i mgul rgyan. The Tai Situ has a copy of this book at his monastery in India. Ka-rma bLo-bzang, the current Gang-dkar sprul-sku's tutor, gave MG a copy during the visit by the present incarnation (yang-srid-pa) to China.

[81] lnga ldan sogs kyi 'bel gtam

[82] A representative from each of five major sDe-dge monasteries: dPal-spungs, Sa-skya dgon-chen, dPal-yul, rDzogs-chen, Kha-tog.

[83] Or, as it was popularly called, "Sakya monastery"

[84] Chogyam Trungpa's monastery

[85] Temple with an image of Tshe-ring dbang-po, the previous Gangkar lama, and his remains.

[86] Temple to Mahakala or mGon-po phyag-bzhi-pa and Ber-nag-can, or mGon-po phyag drug-pa.

[87] Old Tibetan name for Chengdu.

[88] Nyingmapa

[89] Formerly a large Kagyupa monastery, nowadays quite small (MG)

[90] In Yunnan. Great artists came from the many Kagyupa monasteries that are now gone, being replaced by those belonging to the Gelukpa sect (MG).

[91] These offerings were not expected and were outside what could have been thought about or imagined.

[92] sku-'dra, representing the existentiality, communication, and responsive functions of an Awakened Being in the form of a Buddha image, book, and stupa respectively.

[93] This temple is gone. It was a big temple at one time, with five or six monks in residence. The Karmapa Chos-dbyings rdo-rje and Rol-pa'i rdo-rje were benefactors (MG)

[94] The brTson-'grus mthar-phyin yang-srid (incarnation) lives in Kham (MG).

[95] This is a famous pilgrimage place within Minyag territory with three peaks arranged in a triangular pattern (when viewed from the air) dedicated to sPyan-ras-gzigs (Avalokitesvara), Phyag-na rdo-rje (Vajrapani), and 'Jams-pa'i dbyangs (Manjughosa)

[96] Very small retreat, see p 412, Rock.

[97] 'ba'-pa mang-po

[98] English, American, French. One of his American students was George Kraft, author of the recently re-issued Tibetan-English Colloquial Primer (Khams-skad) - Kham Dialect. He was fluent in Chinese and served as a missionary in China for many years before moving to Kangding with his family. There he studied the Kham dialect of Tibetan. He was given the name Nam-mkha'i rgyal-mtshan when he was a student with Tshul-khrims zla-ba. He is fondly remembered to this day in Kham. During a visit to rDzogs-chen monastery in 1999, an elderly monk approached me soon after my arrival there and asked if I knew a Christian teacher name Wangden (dBang-ldan). It took me a moment to remember that Wangden ('Strong One') was the nickname given to George because of his strapping 6 ft. 4in physique. He still had a bone-crushing handshake in the last months of his life. He lived in Kangding and traveled throughout the Kham-Minyag area up to Ganze spreading the Christian gospel. After the Kraft family left China, they moved to California, settling in the East Bay hills. George died in 2002.

[99] Small monastery of about 60 monks. (MG)

[100] rgya ma = 1.1023 pounds

144

[101] As a mKhan-po, "Scholar", Gangkar Rinpoche was skilled in teaching. The title of mKhan-po in the Nyingmapa, Kagyupa, Sakyapa traditions indicates one who is skilled in teaching texts. The Gelukpa does not have an equivalent title associated with specific teaching skill sets. A dGe-shes may be specifically highly skilled at debate and not necessarily at teaching as such.

[102] by 'Jigs-med gling-pa, 1729(30)-1898

[103] The monasteries sKabs 'gar lha sgang, Brag mkhar, Ba ri, Seng ge belonged to the Nyingmapa sect and sKyid gling was a Gelukpa monastery.(MG)

[104] 'Ba - Nyingma monastery in Gartok (MG)

[105] Including the works of the Nyingma master kLong-chen-rab-'byams-pa in the curriculum was a natural outflow of the connection of the Karma bKa'-brgyud lineage with the Nying-ma-pa since the days when the 3rd Karma-pa Rang-byung rdor-rje was kLong-chen-pa's teacher.

[106] Gha.thar-lam, big monastery in Yushu, very good place to study Lam-'bras (the Path and (its) Result) teachings. (MG)

[107] In the biography of Dezhung Rinpoche, "A Saint in Seattle", the time of this visit is given as 1944 or 1945. Dezhung Rinpoche stayed at Gangkar monastery for seven months. He received extensive teachings during his stay there and later would consider Gangkar Rinpoche to be one of his main fundamental (root) teachers. See p. 132-136, 203 David Jackson (2003), A Saint in Seattle, for detail on the teachings he received and pictures of some of the teachers listed in this biography.

[108] The present incarnation lives in Lijiang, is an important, highly influential Kagyupa teacher. (MG)

[109] Khrung ching hri krang

[110] He died in India.(MG)

[111] Peter Goullart, in his description of his meeting with Gangkar Rinpoche at Dartsendo said that "(Gangkar Rinpoche) brought with him a handsome Chinese girl who said she was a Buddhist devotee and acted as his secretary and interpreter. She was fashionably dressed a la Goddess

Kwanyin in a wine-red flowing robe with an appropriate hood which was specially designed for her, she said, in Paris. Thanks to her good manners and looks and efficient stage management, the tour was highly successful both spiritually and financially." (Goullart, p. 29)

[112] mGon-po said he heard that this was so but has no confirmation of it. (MG)

[113] Ya'an used to have a large Chinese monastery. (MG)

[114] Canton, Tib: Kong tung

[115] Summer retreat lasts one month.

[116] The winter retreat lasts three months.

[117] Nyingmapa

[118] Sakyapa

[119] A female student

[120] Krung dbyang Mi rigs slob sgrva

[121] slob dpon chen po (great master)

[122] Krang dByi sun

[123] See Li, An-Che. (1948) rNying-ma-pa: The Early Form of Lamaism. *Journal of the Royal Asiatic Society.* London

[124] Living these days in Lanzhou, Gansu.

[125] Currently living in Chengdu. Highly literate in Tibetan and Chinese.(MG)

[126] Literally yab- "father", who is the teacher or bLa-ma, sras "son" who here is the student (slob-ma), gser zhal "gold presence or face, meaning meeting face to face.

[127] mKha'-khyab rdo-rje

[128] Meaning the Lha-sa area and the monasteries of dGa-ldan, Se-ra, 'Bras-spung.

[129] Minyak blo-bzang yon-tan was one of the few Minyag scholars in Lhasa at the time.

[130] ngos rgya ra can

[131] Technically he wasn't a monk.

[132] The last treasurer, a good friend of MG.

[133] spyi sems: thought of the common good

[134] rim-gro bla-ma

[135] Guomingtang

[136] The information on this part of Rinpoche's life was based on recollections as told to MG by bSod-nams tshe-ring. (MG)

[137] Rva sha chu is the territory or administrative area.

[138] At sPo-po Padma bkod there were many Kagyupa monasteries before 1910.

[139] All Kagyupa monasteries.

[140] Monk soldiers from Se-ra and 'Bras-spungs (MG)

[141] First incidence of alternate spelling of Nor-lha Rinpoche's name. See Tuttle

[142] There is a lot of historical data in Chinese (MG).

[143] There were many relics (ring srel). MG had heard of all these events but never saw the heart himself. (MG)

[144] Equivalent to the completion process in Kagyupa teachings.

[145] Equivalent to the developmental process in Kagyupa teachings.

[146] Division commander of the army at Chongqing.

[147] See Guenther, <u>Kindly Bent to Ease Us</u>

[148] lit: 10,000

[149] Substituting the more common measurement of "dozens" used in the West for the text which reads "tens" (bcu phrag).

[150] He died Sunday, October 15, 2001 in Honolulu at the age of 101.

[151] Tibetan: Cang shis Lu'u hran

[152] The Tibetan text has the words <u>Gangs</u> and <u>dkar</u> (Rinpoche's name) underlined making this poem a reference to the name and qualities of Gangkar Rinpoche.

[153] All of Gangkar Rinpoche's letters were burned during the Cultural Revolution. Some of Shes-rab rgya-mtsho's letters survived and have been reprinted at the bLa-brang bkra-shis dkyil monastery, a place with many scholars. (MG)

[154] MG was only 16 at the time.

[155] The author of the Gangkar biography.

[156] This monastery in Chengdu no longer exists. The site on which it stood now contains many hotels and is in the neighborhood of the Jinjiang Hotel.

147

[157] Kvang lags hva shang

[158] This is a ceremony to authorize practice of what is popularly translated as "consciousness transference", or, more accurately the transformational process techniques for maintaining awareness in the space (bar-do) after death and preceding birth.

[159] Boa zi Fu Xue she (si), very nice, large monastery, not many monks. (MG)

[160] Tibetan: Wen hru'u; a very active Buddhist temple and popular tourist site in Chengdu these days.

[161] sponsoring- 'gan bzhes 'og

[162] Same as Hong U yon

[163] sku zla tha'e tha'e

[164] 'Pha ri, transcription into Tibetan of the Chinese word for a monk: Hoshang.

[165] Very old, now living on Hainan Dao, speaks Guangdong dialect and some Tibetan (MG)

[166] mDo (sutra, direct teachings of Sakyamuni; 'dul ba (vinaya, monastic code); and mdzod (abhidharma, psychology)

[167] Tibetan: gsol mgron phul = za ma sbyin

[168] Rab mdzes mthon-po'i dgon, very large

[169] Lung Yu is the name of the daughter of a political leader in Yunnan. She now lives in the US.

[170] A high official in the Guomingtang who died in 2000 in Taiwan.

[171] The Chinese title is given in Tibetan: Hphu Ja'o Kva Jo Tsha'an shri

[172] MG went back to Minyag. (MG)

[173] Teacher (Chinese translator) some 300 years ago. Many of his books are at sDe-dge.

[174] On the road to Luding (lCags-zam-kha)

[175] formerly Kagyupa

[176] Gelukpa

[177] ibid.

[178] both monasteries of the Sakya school

[179] He still lives in Kunming, is about 80 years old. His wife and children are also living in Kunming. (MG).

[180] During the Tibetan 8th or 9th month the weather is not too bad. These students stayed with wives and children for a year and then left.

[181] Declaration of liberation was made at Dartsendo.(MG)

[182] Now 86. The translator met him during a visit to San Francisco by a delegation of Tibetans from dKar-mdzes in 2000.

[183] Rinpoche was placed under house arrest. He was not allowed to leave and had limited movement within the building.

[184] It is said that during his confinement Rinpoche told his captors that he didn't need anything, that he was perfectly happy where ever he was. Rinpoche's equanimity is but another sign of his deep realization.

[185] lit: in the presence of, spyan sngar

[186] See Bosson, James E., A Treasury of Aphoristic Jewels and the new version by Davenport, John T. Ordinary Wisdom, Sakya Pandita's Treasury of Good Advice, Boston: Wisdom Publications, 2000.

[187] bod kyi brda sprod rig pa

[188] A teacher from sDe-dge (MG)

[189] Ngag-dbang nor-bu was in Beijing during 1962-1963 (MG).

[190] This teacher died at bLa-brang bkra-shis dkyil. He was a reincarnated teacher from that monastery. He visited America once. (MG)

[191] The Karmapa sent a letter to Gangkar Rinpoche requesting a meeting because Gangkar Rinpoche was his tutor.

[192] Many monks requested empowerments from the Karmapa at this time.(MG)

[193] Another enthonement of the current dPal-spungs Tai Situ incarnation occurred in 1954. The current Gangkar incarnation, Karma Lungtok Tenpai Gyaltsen, notes in an email to the translator that "Gangkar Rinpoche was the tutor

of the then young 12th Situ Rinpoche. One day Rinpoche painted an "A" (Tibetan character) on the tip of Situ Rinpoche's tongue which was to symbolize that he was to be the tutor of the young Rinpoche. Likewise, when the 10th incarnation of Gangkar Rinpoche was young, the then older 12th Situ Rinpoche became his teacher."

[194] Chab srid gros mol khang

[195] chos dbyings su bsdus so; Ngag-dbang nor-bu related these final events to MG. This description of Rinpoche's death uses special vocabulary related to meditation techniques in which the body's energy is stabilized through yogic postures. These postures are called the seven points of Vairocana. The vital energy is stabilized and focused attention is relaxed into what transpersonal psychologists term process structures which link or direct vital energies into the ultimate state, here called the "Chos-dbyings" or meaning reality field.

[196] bzhi rgol las 'gul: these four protest campaigns started in 1962

[197] Of these works the 'Phag bstod kyi 'grel pa is in India. The dBu-ma'i mtha-dpyod lta-ba'i yig-'byed is missing. rGyal-rong dGe-bshes Karma Nges-don-gyi dri-lan mKhas pa'i mgul-rgyan is complete. Part of the sPyod-'jug 'grel-pa mjug-ma rdzogs-pa exists. MG has seen the Phar-phyin chos-'khor rnam-bzhag but it was never published. The bKa' bstan-bcos-kyi rnam-bzhag is missing as is the Byams-pa sangs-rgyas yin-min-gyi rnam-bzhag. Both the dNgos brgyad don bdun-cu'i spyi don sum-rtags bsdu don shes-rab sgron-me and the rGyan drug mchog gnyis-kyi bstod -pa in the cycle of "praise works" exist.

[198] Both of these texts exist.

[199] Included as an appendix in this book.

[200] Of these short works by Gangkar Rinpoche the rDo-rje mdud-pa is missing. The rules of conduct for Khams-gsum grags byams-chen chos-'khor gling is still in use. Of dedication prayers, regular prayers, offering prayers, ritual offerings for propitiation purposes (gser skyems) there are

150

not very many remaining. None of the documentation relating to free discussions on various subjects (tshogs bshad 'bel gtam) exists but there are a few official letters (chab shog) that have been found.

[201] In the <u>Sa-skya legs-bshad</u>

[202] A metaphor for Gangkar Rinpoche's writings (MG).

[203] At Nag-chu-kha (MG)

[204] Gelukpa monastery (MG)

[205] From Lhasa

[206] All three of the scholars were from 'Bras-spungs.

[207] At rTa-gon

[208] Called Gangs-dkar dgon-pa.

[209] "Not much can be written about such events" (MG).

[210] First draft translated into English by S. Brinson Aldridge (Karma gSung-rab rgya-mtsho), Metal-Snake Year of the 17th (2001) calendrical cycle, at Beijing.

[211] bkra-shis rtags-brgyad

[212] rgyal-srid sna-bdun

[213] One who has overcome emotional conflicts.

[214] Comment by Gonpo.

[215] Tara's residence

[216] gtor-snod dang sku chos brdabs

[217] grol-ba bzhi-ldan:

[218] The Chinese name for the river is derived from the Minyag name, Nya(g)-rong.

[219] Except for those in Kangding and some parts of Jiulong County who call themselves Buo-ba, from the Minyag word for mountain, 'Bo, pronounced Buo.

[220] Minyag is variously spelled Minyak, Munia, Muya, Miya, Miyak, Menia, Menya, Meaa and so forth. It is pronounced "Meen Yaw", (the "aw" like the "aw" in "jaw") with a very slight "K" or even hard "G" sometimes heard at the end. In Chinese (Sichuan dialect) one hears "Moon Yaw." The most common spelling used nowadays is Minyak and is adopted throughout the text.

[221] An exception to the relative lack of resources on Kham, not counting what one can find in a good university library,

is David Jackson's excellent biography of Dezhung Rinpoche. That book contains much background on the social/political environment of Kham and particularly the region of Minyag Gha, the birthplace of Dezhung Rinpoche, and an original homeland of the Minyag.

[222] Mi-nyag mGon-po, Bod-kyi lo-rgyus rigs-pa'i nang Minyak-gi gnas-tshul dang Minyak skor-gyi ming-tshig 'gar dpyad-pa, <u>Krung-go'i bod-ljongs</u>, Vol 5, 1998, p.21-23.

[223] Dunnell, Ruth W. (1996). The Great State of White and High, Buddhism and State Formation in Eleventh-Century Xia. Honolulu: University of Hawai'i Press, p. xiii

[224] Uralic and Altaic Series, Indiana University, v137, p.1-2

[225] Mi-nag mgon-po, op.cit.

[226] Japanese mountaineering news and photo

[227] Vitali, Roberto (2003). Glimpses of History of the rGya Clan With Reference to Nyang-stod, Lho mon, and Nearby Lands (7th-13th Century), paper delivered at the First International Seminar on Bhutan Studies, Thimphu.

[228] Hummel, Seigbert (2000). On Zhang-zhung. Dharamsala: Library of Tibetan Works and Archives.

[229] See Tuttle, <u>Tibetan Buddhists in the Making of Modern China</u>.

[230] Kepping, K.B, "Min-nia (Tangut) Self-appellation and Self-portraiture in Khara-Khoto Materials", http://kepping.net/pdfs/works/Mi-Nia_Self-appelation.pdf

[231] Private communication from Professor Herbert Guenther who observed that Tibetans had informal trade relations with the Sogdians in the 7th century and Urgyan to the "northwest of Tibet" is possibly reflected in old names such as Urgyanistan used for the eastern part present-day Tajikistan.

[232] See <u>Civilized Shamans</u> by Samuel Geoffrey.

[233] See Leonard Clark, <u>The Marching Wind</u>.

[234] It is interesting to note that Trungpa writes that the first of the Trungpa incarnations was the son of the Minyag king.

[235] Mi-nyag mGon-po, Bod-kyi lo-rgyus rigs-pa'i nang Mi-nyag-gi gnas-tshul dang Mi-nyag skor-gyi ming-tshig 'gar dpyad-pa, <u>Krung-go'i bod-ljongs</u>, Vol 5, 1998, p.21-23.

[236] brDa-dkrol gser-gyi me-long, p. 269, gives sTong-khun as meaning dong-guo ("Eastern country") in Chinese.

[237] ..not counting 2 days spent acclimatizing for higher altitude; September 9-20, 2003

[238] The Kagyu or "Spoken Transmission" gets its name because spiritual practices are taught directly in this lineage, in a one-on-one contact. It traces its beginnings to a farmer-scholar-layman named Marpa Chokyi Lodro (1012-1097). He is popularly called Marpa the Translator because he translated many books that he brought back from India following his study with Buddhist masters. Some of Marpa's early "notebooks" in his own handwriting still exist. Marpa lived in Lho-drak near the Sikkim border, which has a pleasant climate suitable for growing fruit and other crops. Because Marpa was a married layman-scholar with children, working for a living and modestly successful in investments, he is one of the closest to the heart of many lay practitioners in Tibet who cannot follow the path of the monk or hermit.

[239] Wilson, E.H. A Naturalist in Western China, London: Methuen & Co. Ltd, 1913, p.210-213. Wilson was in Dartsendo during these events.

[241] *sa-bde-chus*, pronounced exactly the same as *sa-sde-chus* above but with different spelling

Bibliography

Tibetan Sources

dGe-'dun chos-'phel et. al 1998. *gNas yig phyogs bsgrigs.* Sichuan: Si khron mi rigs dpe skrun khang

Seng-ge bzang-po. 1987. *Mi nyag mkhas dbang lnga'i rnam thar.* Sichuan, China: Mi rigs dpe skrun khang

Mi-nyag mGon-po. 1997. *'Bo gangs dkar sprul sku'i rnam thar dad pa'i pad dkar.* Beijing: Mi rigs dpe skrun khang

Mi-nyag mGon-po. 1996. *Gangs can mkhas dbang rim byon gyi rnam thar mdor bdsus.* Beijing: Krung go'i bod kyi shes rig dpe skrun khang

Mi-nyag mGon-po. 1991. *bKa' dang bstan bcos 'gyur ro cog bod du byung ba'i tshul mdor tsam brjod pa.* Bod kyi shes rig zhib 'jug ched rtsom bdam bsgrigs, (2), Beijing: Mi rigs dpe skrun khang

dGa-ba'i rdo-rje. 1995. *'Khrungs dpe dri med shel gyi me long.* Beijing: Mi rigs dpe skrun khang

Krang, dByi sun.1985. *Bod rgya tshig mdzod chen mo.* Beijing: Mi rigs dpe skrun khang

Ko zhul grags pa 'byung gnas and rGyal ba blo bzang mkhas grub. 1992. *Gangs can mkhas grub rim byon ming mdzod.* Xining: mTsho sngon mi rigs par khang

bTson-'grus rab-rgyas (ed). 1999. *Krung go bod kyi rig gnas sgyus rtsal kun 'dus zhal thang chen mo'i rnam bshad mthong grol kun gsal me long.* Beijing: Mi rigs dpe skrun khang

'Gyur-med bde-chen.1982 reprint of sDe dge edition. *dPal grub pa'i dbang phyug brtson 'grus bzang po'i rnam par thar pa kun gsal nor bu'i me long.* Si khron: Mi rigs dpe skrun khang

154

'Gos lo gzhon nu dpal. 1984 reprint. *Deb ther sngon po.* Si khron: Mi rigs dpe skrun khang (2 volumes)

dPal 'byor bzang-po (ed). 1985. "Mi nyag rgyal rabs" in *rGya mdzod yig tsang chen mo.* Si-khron: Mi rigs dpe skrun khang

Non-Tibetan Sources

Aris, Michael. 1992. *Lamas, Princes, and Brigands*: Joseph Rock's Photographs of the Tibetan Borderland of China. New York: China House Galley

Bellezza, J.V. 1997. *Divine Dyads, Ancient Civilization in Tibet.* Dharamsala, India: Library of Tibetan Works & Archives

Bosson, James E. 1969. *A Treasury of Aphoristic Jewels,* The Subhasitaratnasidhi of Sa Skya Pandita in Tibetan and Mongolian, Bloomington, Indiana: Indiana University

Burdsall, Richard L. and Moore, Terris, "Climbing Mighty Minya Konka, Landmark of China's New Skyway, *The National Geographic Magazine,* May, 1943 (Vol. LXXXIII, No. 5, p. 625-650), Washington, D.C., The National Geographic Society, 1943.

Chang, C.C. 1961. *Esoteric Teachings of the Tibetan Tantra.* Falcon's Wing Press

Chang, Garma C.C. 1963. *Six Yogas of Naropa & Teachings on Mahamudra.* Ithica, N.Y.: Snow Lion Publications

Csome de Koros, Alexander.1916. *Sanskrit-Tibetan-English Vocabulary*: Being an Edition and Translation of the Mahavyupatti. Calcutta: Memoirs of the Asiatic Society of Bengal, Vol. IV, No. 2, pp.129-251

Dorje, Gyurme.1966. *Tibet Handbook with Bhutan.* Chicago, Illinois: Passport Books

Dunnell, Ruth W.1996. *The Great State of White and High,* Buddhism and State Formation in Eleventh-Century Xia, Honolulu: University of Hawai'i Press

Edou, J. 1996. *Machig Labdron and the Foundations of Chod.* Ithica, New York: Snow Lion Publications

Goullart, Peter. 1959. *Princes of the Black Bone*, Life in the Tibetan Borderland. London: John Murray

Jackson, David.2003. *A Saint in Seattle. The Life of the Tibetan Mystic Dezhung Rinpoche.* Boston: Wisdom Publications

Li, An-Che. 1948. *"rNying-ma-pa: The Early Form of Lamaism". Journal of the Royal Asiatic Society.* London

Lue, Kwanten and Hesse, Susan.1980. *Tangut (His Hsia) Studies: A Bibliography.* Bloomington, Indiana: Research Institute for Inner Asian Studies, Uralic and Altaic Series, Vol. 137

Luk, Charles.1988. (Translator): *Empty Cloud, The Autobiography of the Chinese Zen Master Xu Yun.* Dorset, England: Element Books

Muses, C.A.(ed).**1961.**, *Esoteric Teachings of the Tibetan Tantra,* including seven initiation rituals and the *Six Yogas of Naropa* in Tsong-Kha-pa's commentary translated by Chang Chen Chi, former lecturer at the Kong-ka lamasery, Meinya, East Tibet. Falcon's Wind Press

Rock, J.R., "The Glories of the Minya Konka." *The National Geographic Magazine.* October, 1930 (Vol. LVIII, No. 4, p.385-487), Washington, D.C., The National Geographic Society

Rock, Joseph F., "Konka Risumgongba, Holy Mountain of the Outlaws", *The National Geographic Magazine*, July, 1931 (Vol. LX, No. 1, p. 1-65), Washington, D.C., The National Geographic Society

Rockhill, William Woodville 1977. *Notes on Tibet.* New Delhi: Asian Publication Services

Roerick, George N. 1976. *The Blue Annals.* Delhi: Motilal Banarsidass

Stein, R.A. 1972. *Tibetan Civilization.* Stanford, California: Stanford University Press

Taylor, McComas and Yuthok, Lama Chodak (translators).1996. *The Clear Mirror*. A traditional account of Tibet's Golden Age (Sakyapa Sonam Gyaltsen (1312-1375), "Clear Mirror on Royal Geneology"). Ithica, New York. Snow Lion Publications

Teichman, Eric.1922. *Travels of a Consular Officer in Eastern Tibet, together with a History of the Relations between China, Tibet and India*. Cambridge: At the University Press

Vitali, Roberto.1996. *The Kingdoms of Gu.ge Pu.hrang According to Mnga'.ris rgyal.rabs of Gu.ge.mkhan.chen.Ngag.dbang.grags.pa*. Dharamsala: Tho.ling.gtsug.lag.khang.lo.gcig.stong.'khor.ba'i.rjes.dran.m dzad.sgo'i.go.sgrig.tshogs.drung

Wissing, Douglas A. 2004. *Pioneer in Tibet*. The Life and Perils of Dr. Albert Shelton. New York: Palgrave MacMillan

Zangpo, Ngawang.2001. *Sacred Ground, Jamgon Kontrul on "Pilgrimage and Sacred Geography"*. Ithica, New York: Snow Lion Publications

Suggest reading (Tibetan history):

Goldstein, Melvyn C. 1989. *A History of Modern Tibet, 1913-1951*. The Demise of the Lamaist State. Berkeley: University of Californian Press

Kapstein, Matthew T. 2005. *The Tibetan Assimulation of Buddhism*, Conversion, Contestation, and Memory. Oxford: Oxford University Press

Snellgrove, David and Richardson, Hugh.1986. *A Cultural History of Tibet*. Boston: Shambhala Publications, Inc.

Stein, R.A. 1972. *Tibetan Civilization*. Stanford, California: Stanford University Press

Glossary of terms used in translation

Sanskrit

bodhisattva - one who works toward the awakening of all beings

dakini - energetic thoughtforms in female form, evocative of the movement of energy in space, symbols of the naked or natural mind or *rigpa* stripped of all obscuration and defilements.

dharma - teachings of the Buddha

dharini - longer form of a mantra

madyamika - Tibetan -dbu-ma, the central view - meaning not holding any extreme views, especially those of eternalism or nihilism.

mahamudra - Buddhist method of direct introduction to the nature and essence of Mind (or Buddha-nature) and the practice of stabilizing the accompanying transcendental realization

mani - short term for the mantra to Avalokitesvara: Om Mani Padme Hung.

mantra - religious or mystical syllable or poem, used to help focus the mind in meditation

nirvana - end to worldly suffering, the opposite of worldly existence (samsara)

prajnaparamita - a genre of Mahayana Buddhist scriptures dealing with the subject of the Perfection of Wisdom. The term Prajñāpāramitā alone never refers to a specific text, but always to the class of literature.

puja - prayers and rituals

sadhana - spiritual practice including chanting, meditation, yoga, etc.

siddha - one who is accomplished, has achieved realization in spiritual practice stupa - reliquary, called a pagoda in China, holding relics of the Buddha or Buddhist saints

sunyata - often translated as emptiness or voidness; signifies that everything one encounters in life is empty of absolute identity, permanence, or an in-dwelling 'self'. This is because everything is inter-related and mutually dependent - never wholly self-sufficient or independent.

sutra - Buddhist texts assumed to be the recorded sayings of the historical Buddha

tantra - a set of documents and techniques that codify or structure complex spiritual practices intended to lead to the direct experience of one's true nature

Tibetan

khregs-chod - "cutting through;" total relaxation, the dissolving of tensions, the fundamental practice of integrating the state of contemplation into daily activity. In it, all the tensions of body, voice and mind linked to tendencies of which one is unaware dissolve without effort, liberating themselves.

thig-le - dot, vibrating focal point; red and white vital energy shared by both males and females

thod-rgal - "leaping high", or "crossing over"; quantum leap, method of contemplation of light by which rdzogs-chen practitioners attain the 'ja' lus (rainbow biody) without leaving mortal remains at death

phyag-chen -Tibetan for Mahamudra

'pho-ba - transformation processes at death

'pho-lung - permission to practice specific techniques that will enable control over the processes experienced at death

rtsa - pathways in which vital energy (qi) moves within the body

rlung - vital energy controlled through breath

lus sbyong - physical exercises

'od-gsal - clear light, lucidity, regarded as the true nature of mind

Author's Biography

Gonpo was born in 1923 at Sadan in Minyak Ringmo, near Gonga Shan. Driven by poverty, he was taken to the Gangkar monastery when he was five. At the time it was widely accepted that if one became a monk, the aims of both this life and the next would be achieved and great merit would result. Gonpo was given the name Karma bSod-nam rgya-mtsho by the 5th Gangkar Lama. He first learned to read and write while under the care of a maternal uncle who was used to a life devoted to just meditation and recitation of prayers. Seven years passed during which Gonpo learned all the prayers and rituals in the monastery.

In 1937, when he was 14, he was able to attend the first school completed that year at Gangkar monastery. He studied the five traditional branches of knowledge (grammar, logic, craftsmanship, healing, and spirituality). Gonpo's mother had been supporting his monastic life financially. She died soon after he graduated from the school when he was 25.

In 1946, he traveled with Gangkar Rinpoche to Chengdu and Chongqing in Sichuan Province and Kunming in Yunnan. After seeing the world outside, he left the monastery. In 1951, Kangding was liberated. With other workers he created a class in school to provide training for teachers. He started his work compiling the best speeches of Gangkar Rinpoche. He then went to work for the Kangding Culture and Education Bureau, translating and editing many textbooks. He also began teaching Tibetan writing to Han cadres and introducing them to various characteristics of Tibetan culture. He moved to the Southwest Minorities University and was a supervisor by 1956. In 1963, when he was 40, Gonpo married Chodron (Chos-sgron), the daughter of a teacher at the Minorities University.

Three years later, in 1966, China was engulfed in the chaos of the Cultural Revolution. Because he had been a student of Gangkar Rinpoche, he was put in prison for seven months and frequently beaten. Gonpo's training in rtsa-lung, similar to qigong breathing exercises, helped him get through the prison experience as he could transform his difficulties through his rtsa-rlung practice.

He was released after 7 months but was assigned to work as a carpenter and cook in a forestry farm near Kangding. In 1977, when another correction to Communist Party policies was made, he was again made an editor of textbooks at the Culture and Education House. Then, in 1979, he was transferred to work with the Nationalities Translation Bureau. Gonpo's knowledge of economics and political science increased from the thorough exposure to Western ideas during this period of his life while working as a translator.

In 1980, he was invited to the People's Culture Palace and began work in cataloguing ancient Tibetan texts. These were libraries of texts from major monasteries moved from Tibet after 1959 for safe-keeping. Gonpo was happy with this work with Tibetan national treasures. In 1984, he moved to working at the Minorities National Library, continuing to work with other collections of Tibetan texts. He edited and wrote sections of four of the catalogues of texts at the library printed to date. In 1994, many books removed from Tibet were returned.

Though he is officially retired, Gonpo continues to write, teach, serve as a member of committees at the Center for Chinese Tibetology Research, work on new projects at the Minorities Library, and have meetings with Tibetologists from overseas. His recent book is on the structural pathways (rtsa) and vital energy (rlung), Tibetan rtsa-rlung as a science.

Translator's biography

S. Brinson Aldridge was born and raised in Vermont. When he was in college he met his first Buddhist teachers, monks belonging to Chinese and Korean Chan traditions. He began learning Tibetan to understand the concepts used in describing states of awareness in Buddhist meditation and its underlying philosophy as found in the original texts. After college at the University of Pennsylvania, he read Tibetan with Radha Chime Rinpoche in London. During travels to Nepal, India and Sikkim in 1976, he attended lectures at Tibetan Buddhist monasteries and studied with Karmapa Rang-byung Rig-pa'i rDo-rje, Khra'-'gu Rinpoche, bsTan-dga' Rinpoche, mKhan-po brTson-'grus and other teachers in the Kagyu-Nyingma lineages. After returning to the States, he studied with David Snellgrove at U.C Berkeley, H.V. Guenther, and Hiroshi Sonami (Ngor Thar-brtse mKhan-po bSod-nams rGya-mtsho). He continues to work with Tibetan teachers.

Brinson's interest in Buddhist meditation and pilgrimage has been strongly influenced by Tibetan traditions that developed out of the convergence of Tibetan and Chinese approaches to meditation. The translation of the biography of Gangkar Rinpoche is one of several ongoing projects inspired by meetings with monks, nuns, and hermits while on pilgrimage to mountain temples, caves, and monasteries in China, sites sacred in Chinese and Tibetan Buddhist traditions.

When he is not off on retreat or pilgrimage, Brinson lives in Northern California with his family and works as a network specialist in the health care industry.

Postscript

It is sad to report that Gonpo passed away in late April, 2008, following a sudden illness. He was 85 years old. I regret he was not able to see a copy of this book in print before his death.

Index

Printed in Great Britain
by Amazon